GREEN VALLEY

❧ The Heart Of Green Valley Series ❧

GREEN VALLEY

Meredith Resce

Authentic
MEDIA

Authentic Media
We welcome your comments and questions.
129 Mobilization Drive, Waynesboro, GA 30830 USA
authenticusa@stl.org
and 9 Holdom Avenue, Bletchley, Milton Keynes, Bucks, MK1 1QR, UK
www.authenticbooks.com

If you would like a copy of our current catalog, contact us at:
1-8MORE-BOOKS
ordersusa@stl.org

Green Valley
ISBN: 1-932805-32-X

First published in 1998 by Golden Grain Publishing
PO Box 93, O'Halloran Hill, SA5158, Australia

09 08 07 06 05   6 5 4 3 2 1

Published in 2005 by Authentic Media

Cover design: Paul Lewis

Printed in Colombia

To my mother
Jennette Bishop

The woman who made me believe
that I could achieve just about anything
if only I would have a go at it.

ABOUT THE AUTHOR

Meredith Resce was born and raised in the Southern Flinders Ranges of South Australia, in the community of Melrose.

Meredith and her husband Nick have worked in the ministry for eighteen years, having served a six year period in Geelong, Victoria. They now work with Southside Christian Church in Adelaide, South Australia.

Meredith has completed a Bible College Certificate Course and also a certificate course in psychology. Apart from writing, Meredith Resce lectures to groups on various subjects including development of relationship skills and growth toward emotional health.

She has three teenage children, Elisa, David and Michael.

CHAPTER 1

Green Valley, Rural Victoria, Australia, 1886

C olin gently nudged his horse into motion, sighing to himself as he moved away from the house. It was getting close to dark and he knew that he should have left for home some time ago, but the lure of friendship had kept him from doing what he should have done.

He didn't turn to look back at Ned's small dwelling once he was underway. He already had enough regrets without pining over his friend's blessings, each one reminding him of how lonely he really was.

But it was as if even this thought was forbidden as he determinedly shook it from his mind. *I have a mother, four sisters and a brother at home. Why on earth am I carrying on like this?* He asked the question of himself, and just as quickly he knew the answer. Having spent the day with his closest friend, Ned, then having shared an early dinner with him and his family, had made Colin realise the emptiness there was inside him – the longing for close companionship.

It was no use recalling the many occupants of his own small house. He knew only too well how many of them there were. After all, hadn't he been the one who had been responsible for feeding and clothing them for the last five years?

Ever since his father had been killed, just before his sixteenth birthday, Colin had taken on the duties and burden of working the land that had been left for them. His mother had fretted and worried that the task would be too much for one so young, but Colin was determined to succeed.

It wasn't just the fact that his mother, sisters and brother would starve if he didn't achieve success, more than that, it was his pride. He might only have been sixteen at the time, but he was old enough to know what it meant to fail – and that was something that he had no intention of doing.

In the early days following his father's death, many neighbours and friends had offered their help and advice. Admittedly Colin was proud, but he was not so stupid as to refuse this much needed input. One man in particular had been a tower of strength to him in the most difficult times, and that was the parish minister. John Laslett had proved himself not only as a preacher and pastor, but also as a man who was willing to put legs on his faith – to practise what he preached, as it were. He had swung an axe, herded cattle and swung a scythe in rhythm with the sound words of wisdom and comfort he offered as he worked. Colin admired and respected the man.

Ned Miller was another man who had earned Colin Shore's trust and confidence. Ned was several years older than Colin, and had married his wife, Lilly, not long after the elder Mr Shore had died. Being young and out on his own, Ned seemed to have a depth of understanding as to what it was like to be setting out alone against the world.

Ned's concern for Colin was increased as he knew the heavy responsibility the young boy shouldered having to look after his mother and siblings. And so Ned did all he could to befriend the grieving young man. He carefully built a friendship with him, and it had grown to a point where the two co-operated on a number of projects. They shared investments on expensive farm equipment. They worked together on particularly hard jobs. Over the five years, Colin had as much a place by their fire as he did by his own.

He expelled another breath as he thought about the Miller cabin. It was not a grand house by any means, no more than his own. It was not its structure that held any charm, but rather its occupants and their daily lives. In their five years of marriage, Lilly Miller had produced two children, and was even now expecting a third. Far be it from Ned to complain about another mouth to feed, as Colin had privately thought on many occasions. But then Colin already had seven mouths to feed. No. Ned saw his babies as a blessing, and boasted over each one in turn. Sometimes Colin envied him; sometimes he was relieved that there was no more chance of adding to the number in his own household.

But it was the relationship that Ned shared with Lilly that tore at Colin more than anything. It was the same when Colin observed the Reverend and Mrs Laslett. He didn't understand it, but he knew that it had more appeal than a house full of sisters, and a young brother not long out of nappies.

Ned had hinted and joked with Colin on a number of occasions. He had made it quite clear that he would be happy to match the young farmer up with his own sister, Kathleen Miller. Colin had smiled good-naturedly, but didn't give it any serious thought. The couple of times Kathleen had crossed his mind, Colin tried to imagine how she would fit in in his crowded house and, just as quickly, he dismissed the thought. Even if the eldest of his sisters did get married – as his mother very much hoped – there would still be more females in the house than were really necessary. Mrs Shore was only just forty, and still quite capable of running the household and garden on her own. Yet with her there was Julianne, Christine, Samantha and June. Colin shook his head in disgust again. There were too many women in that one small kitchen already. To bring in yet another one would be excessive.

Lilly Miller had spoken on the subject only once, and it was at that time that she had suggested that if he really loved a woman enough, it wouldn't really matter to him or to her. But that was just it. Colin didn't really think that he even liked Kathleen very much, let alone loved her.

Colin broke from his melancholy thoughts as he saw the silhouette of his house in the distance. *I'm only twenty-one, for goodness sake*, he recited to himself. *There is no rush for me to get married*.

Even as Colin tended to his animal – taking off the harness, rubbing the horse's coat down; measuring him out some oats – he continued with the thought of marriage. *There's no rush for me to get married*, he repeated to himself, *but the sooner Pete Browning makes up his mind and takes Julianne off my hands the better it will be*.

Colin didn't stop to think how cool and calculating his attitude was toward his sister and her suitor. If he had bothered to think further than his own responsibilities, he would have remembered that Pete was one of twelve children, seven of them younger sisters. But even then, Colin would have justified that because he knew the other young man intended to set out further from Green Valley to buy land of his own. Pete Browning only waited for his next younger brother to be of an age to be capable of taking on his share of the load. There was not much doubt in Colin's mind that as soon as Jack Browning turned sixteen, Pete would marry Julianne, and the folk of Green Valley would no longer see them.

Looking forward to that day with an unreasonable anticipation, Colin closed the stable door and headed towards the house.

'How are you, Col?' Before Colin could step inside, he was greeted by the very person he had been thinking about.

'Hello, Pete.' Colin tried not to show the impatience that had coloured his thoughts. 'You got up the courage to ask her yet?'

Pete smiled at the brother's matter-of-fact approach.

'I asked her ages ago, my friend. You don't have to worry about that. My intentions are purely honourable.'

'I knew that!' Colin revealed his shame at having been misunderstood. 'I've just been wondering when you would actually get about the job of getting married.'

'You make it sound like a distasteful chore.' Pete was not about to have the shine taken off of his romantic prospects.

'I'm surprised at you, Pete. I'd have thought that with seven sisters you'd have had enough of female company.'

At that point, Julianne stepped out onto the veranda, the light from inside spilling out with her. 'Oh, it's you, Col. Mum was wondering when you would finally get home. You been out seeing Kathleen?'

'No! I have not!' Colin was instantly defensive.

'Sorry!' Julianne held her hands up in mock apology. 'Must have had an argument with her.' She whispered this comment as an aside to Pete, but Colin heard it. He tried to contain his annoyance with the pair of them, but made a poor job of it.

'I'll see you again.' He offered the parting words to Pete with apparent indifference before he moved inside.

'You'd better not taunt him, Julianne,' Pete counselled.

'Why? What's bothering him?' Julianne didn't seem particularly generous toward her brother.

'I don't know, but he's obviously feeling bad about something. Almost seems as if he's jealous that we have each other. Maybe he's not happy with you getting married.'

'Col! Not happy with me getting married! Now that's very funny, Pete,' Julianne seemed half-serious in the comment. 'Colin has been on edge for ages, always asking if I know when we'll be leaving. If I didn't know better, I'd say he was eager to get rid of me.'

'That couldn't be it, surely,' Pete sounded concerned. 'You've always got on all right, haven't you?'

'We've had our ups and downs the same as most families do, but lately, he has been acting kind of funny.'

'Perhaps seeing us just makes his singleness seem more lonely. He'd never admit to it, of course.'

'Perhaps. Though I thought that Lilly Miller had hinted of her sister-in-law being a hopeful prospect for him.'

'Maybe he doesn't like Kathleen.'

'Maybe not, but then, beggars can't be choosers, can they?'

The couple on the veranda failed to make any sense of Colin's odd behaviour, but then the man himself was unable to come up with a feasible excuse for his less than tolerant attitude either. Having greeted his mother and other sisters cleaning up the kitchen following dinner, he felt his annoyance increase.

'Did you and Ned get the sheep sorted?' Mrs Shore was oblivious to her son's internal struggle.

'Yeah!' Colin did not bother to elaborate.

'How many are you going to take to the market?' the mother persisted.

'Ned has about twenty, and I've got fifteen that are ready.'

'They in good condition? Will they fetch a reasonable price?'

'I don't know, Mum!' Colin's answers continued to be short and lacking affection. 'Look, I'm a bit tired. I think I'll turn in early.'

Mrs Shore didn't bother to reprimand her son for his rudeness. She had stopped looking at him as one of the children some years back. Colin had risen quickly to the position of 'man of the house' and though it had not been easy, Mrs Shore had learned to defer to her son's strengths in leadership.

Now, as she watched him leave the small kitchen, she wondered what it was that had put him out of sorts. She sighed with regret as she hung up the dishtowel. She knew that he must be frustrated, having lost his youth to a premature role of responsibility. Rose Shore had battled with this thought constantly in the last five years. *Perhaps I should have remarried*, she thought to herself, not for the first time.

At the time that her husband had been killed, Rose had been too devastated to consider remarriage. Then, gradually, as the pain had eased, she saw the burden that had been placed on her young son, and she felt it was her duty to marry, if only to relieve Colin of the pressure. But sadly, the only opportunity that presented itself was that of a middle-aged man, not known to anyone in the Valley.

At first, Rose thought that Samuel Jones might have been an answer to their desperate situation. She could not find any love for him in her heart, but she would have married him out of duty for her young family. She shuddered with revulsion at the memories of that time. If it hadn't have been for the reverend – his strong caution and recommendation to wait – Rose could easily have been destroyed by the violence of a man she did not know. She might have found herself legally married to Samuel Jones, who later proved to be an alcoholic with definite tendencies towards physical abuse. Rose experienced his brutality at firsthand, when she suggested that they should not rush into a marriage. He had exploded in a fit of anger, and the fury lasted long enough to reveal how he would treat anyone who dared oppose him. Rose, herself, had been slapped across the face, and when Colin had come to her aid, Samuel had taken to him like a bull to a red rag. Colin nursed a number of injuries as a result of the incident.

Despite the horror of the event, Rose was thankful that she had found out before the wedding, and that she had been able to summon the help of neighbours to see Samuel Jones safely out of their lives.

Since then, Rose had not been particularly eager to find another man to marry. But now Colin was no longer a boy – he was a man of marriageable age. Rose knew that he must harbour some thoughts of this nature. All of his friends were married, even though they were a little older. And with one younger sister all but given away in wedlock, he could not possibly ignore the possibilities for himself.

Rose thought she knew how he must feel. Their house was only small. They had the kitchen where they cooked, ate and sat around the fire. Other than this room, there was one bedroom that Rose shared with her four daughters, and a small lean-to sleepout that Colin shared with his seven-year-old brother, Harry. Rose knew that Colin could not possibly have time or resources to build a house of his own. As it was, the little they earned off the land was scarcely enough to support the seven of them.

Rose's thoughts argued with her. On the one hand she wanted to release her son from the obligation of caring for his mother and siblings. She wanted to set him free to seek a life, a wife and family of his own. But the other part of her thoughts would not, could not, allow these ideas free expression. There was no other way for Rose to care for her other daughters and young son: Colin had to stay with them. The dilemma ate at the mother's heart.

God, I wish there were another way, she prayed.

Yet another wave of guilt washed over Emily as she took in the scene before her. Emily's father, Earl Stanford Wallace, lay listlessly on the divan, seemingly spent of all energy. Emily struggled with the thoughts that threatened not only to accuse her, but to judge and execute her as well. It was her fault that her father was sprawled helplessly, unable to do anything for himself, and unable to undertake any of his normal duties.

If only I could do as he asks. This lament went on over and over in Emily's mind. But each time, she came back to the same stalemate conclusion, and each time the subject came up between them she took the same emotional stand she had just come away from. She simply could not bring herself to agree to her father's request. No matter how much argument and emotional turmoil it caused, Emily would never be able to fulfil his desire. And now, as a result of their most recent argument on the matter, her father had had a relapse.

It's all my fault, Emily cried out in her heart again. *I know he is sick. Why can't I just say yes?* She turned away from looking at him and moved out of the room into the hallway. The misery of the internal conflict showed very clearly on her face, accentuated by the two tears that had escaped, and now rolled unchecked down her cheek.

'Have you settled everything with father?' Emily was startled from her thoughts by her brother's question.

'Settled?' She asked the question, knowing full well what he meant, yet not having the answer she knew he would require.

'Can I go back to Lord Derickson with your decision?' He asked almost impatiently.

Emily paused, her stomach knotted with the anxiety of expecting another verbal battle.

'When can we set the wedding date, Emily? For goodness sake! Why are you being so stubborn about this?'

'There won't be any wedding, Charles,' Emily spoke the denial out with conviction. Her brother had pushed her to the point of anger, just as her father had done moments before. 'I have no wish to marry Lord Derickson, nor anyone related to him.'

'No one related to him has made any offer, child.' Charles' voice rose in authority. He was eight years older than his younger sister, and didn't have any bother treating her as if she were his daughter. 'Lord Derickson has made a most generous offer, and I cannot think of any reason why you should not be extremely grateful.'

'Lord Derickson is nearly sixty years old!' Emily began to recite her objections again. 'I am not quite seventeen. He has been married twice before. Why must I throw myself away on an old man?'

'What! I suppose you think you could make a better match on your own. Emily, you need to do as you are told, and trust me when I tell you this is for your own security and future.'

'But Charles, I am afraid of him. Don't you understand that?'

'Don't be ridiculous,' Charles snorted. 'What's there to be afraid of?'

'It's the way he looks at me. I hate the look in his eye. And if he's anything like his son, then I have good reason to be worried.'

'His son! What have you had to do with *him*? Emily, I hope you haven't any designs on Frederick Derickson. He is married, you know?'

'He may be married, but it hasn't stopped him from making bold advances toward me whenever he finds me alone. I'm so afraid of the pair of them that I barricade myself in my room when I know they are on the grounds.'

'You do make up such terrible stories, Emily.' Charles seemed unconvinced by all her claims.

'Don't you believe me, Charles?' she asked, panic beginning to rise in her throat. 'I do believe that neither Frederick nor his father would have any scruples about . . .' She swallowed the thought, unable to voice the fear that had haunted her for so many months.

'Well, if you would just marry the man, then he wouldn't need to lust after you, would he?'

'Charles!' Emily fully expressed her shock at the coarseness of her brother's comment.

'Emily, please grow up! All you need to do is produce Derickson another son, and then you can have as many affairs as you choose. He probably won't care one way or the other. All he wants is an alliance with our family, which would very much help the Wallace family reputation, and then there will be a son to pass our mother's estate on to now that it has been left entirely to you.'

'I won't listen to you any more, Charles.' Emily indicated her intentions by placing her hands over her ears, and turning to walk away. She was shocked and hurt by her brother's attitude. At least her father had not talked in such a base manner. At least he had tried to promote the marriage as a decent and honourable match.

Yet, as Emily thought further on it, once safely back in her room, she had to admit that Charles had clearly defined all of her previously unidentified fears. He had not denied that Lord Derickson or his son, Frederick were anything other than philanderers. She did not know for certain, but she had heard rumours of the kind of immoral behaviour that Charles had suggested. She knew that she was innocent in the ways of the world, and was not entirely ungrateful for that fact. She tried to pretend that her brother was a decent-living gentleman, but she was finding it harder and harder to deny the suspicions that kept provoking her. While her father had been sick the past few months, Charles had brought any number of strange women to Wallace Hall. Emily had never been introduced to them, as she was sure she should have been if they had been well-bred ladies. The whole sickening truth began to take form in her mind, and the more she considered it, the more she wanted to run and hide.

By the time it was her hour for bed, Emily had worked herself into a proper state of panic. When her father had made the initial suggestion, Emily had understood that the marriage would benefit both families financially, and that it would be a good thing for all concerned. But since her father's illness, Charles had become more insistent about it. Emily had never liked the proposal, but even less now, having seen firsthand just what manner of man Lord Richard Derickson was. Yet Charles seemed to be assuming his father's authority, and with it trying to force the disgusting situation upon his young sister. Stanford Wallace was so ill that he had almost lost any will to fight, either his daughter or his son. *At least Father won't force me against my will*, Emily thought. *But Charles will, if he gets half a chance*.

And this was the thought that remained foremost in her mind. There was only one small hope left open to her, and even that seemed terrifying. Emily remembered her father saying – more as a threat than anything else: 'If you refuse to obey me, Emily, I will send you out to your aunt in Australia. Perhaps then you will learn to appreciate the life you have here. Once you are stuck in that god-forsaken country amongst convicts, you will soon learn to mind.'

Now, as Emily recalled the warning, she began to think of it as a possibility of escape. Her father's younger brother, Lord Jamieson Wallace, had taken his bride and emigrated to the other side of the world some thirty years ago. Emily recalled hearing of her uncle's death, though it had happened many years before she was even born. Nobody referred much to the aunt who remained, but Emily knew her name: Lady Vera Wallace.

'Perhaps living amongst convicts on a desert island will not be as bad as what Charles and Father have planned for me here,' Emily whispered to herself, the thought rapidly becoming a concrete plan in her heart.

CHAPTER 2

Many emotions threatened to swamp Emily as she heard the announcement being shouted below deck. From her stateroom she could clearly hear the clamour of excitement that rose as other passengers readied themselves to go above deck, hopeful for a glance at the new land which they were approaching.

'Aren't you going to come with us, Emily?' The question was asked by a Mrs Manley, Emily's companion and chaperone for the trip.

'No! I think I will wait until we have docked and are ready to disembark.' Emily tried to sound confident, in spite of the fear she felt. Emily waited for her companion as she listed off the many reasons why she should take this opportunity before offering another weak denial, hoping to be left alone to think.

The whole prospect of even taking this trip had terrified the young lady, yet she had forged ahead with the plans in the face of the awful alternative. Her father had dismissed the affair with a cursory nod. 'Perhaps the time away will do you good, child.' He was weak with the sickness when he had spoken, and Emily knew that he could no longer manage any force behind his emotional decisions.

Of course, her brother, Charles, had raved in anger at the idea. He had insisted that Emily stop her whining and prepare herself for the wedding. But Charles' ranting was nothing without their father's authority; even the arrogant brother knew that.

And so, Emily Wallace had booked her passage, engaged the services of Mrs Manley, who was emigrating to be with her family, and overseen the packing of her trunks. During all the time of preparation, Emily tried not to think of what such a voyage actually meant. She just went through the motions, as if she were going no farther than an outing in the park.

By the time she had left her father's house, she knew it was too late to turn back. Earl Stanford Wallace was too ill to really care whether his daughter came or went. Really, it was Charles' continual threats and attempts to bully her that compelled her to keep going.

Once out to sea, there was no turning back no matter how Emily's heart cried out in fear and sadness. It took only two or three days for her to find her sea legs, and then Emily had all the time in the world to consider the choice she had made, and the probable consequences, and the more she considered, the more depressed she became. If she had felt there would have been any benefit, she would have demanded the captain turn the ship around and head back to England. There might have been misery in her homeland, but at least it was familiar and had a measure of security about it.

Now, with just about every human being aboard on deck welcoming the sight of Port Melbourne, Emily dropped her head in her hands and allowed all of her anguish expression as she sobbed from deep inside her.

Colin knew that it was time for him to talk. He had been stewing over his frustrations for long enough, and even he could recognise the tension that existed in his household because of it. He had set out in the morning with the express purpose of catching his friend, the Reverend John Laslett, before that gentleman set out on pastoral visits for the day.

But when he arrived at the manse, Colin found that John was not about to set out on pastoral duties – at least not locally.

'Come in, Colin.' Kate Laslett had smiled and welcomed the young farmer in, offering him a cup of tea as she did so. 'Everything is all right with your mother, I hope?' Kate voiced her concern the moment it crossed her mind.

'Yes! Yes, my mother's fine.' Colin discharged the information without zeal. 'I was hoping that I would be in time to catch your husband before he goes out for the day.'

'You're in plenty of time,' Kate smiled. 'John won't be going out today as he's getting ready to go to the city tomorrow.'

'The city?' Colin was surprised.

'Yes!' Kate continued in explanation. 'Lady Vera has asked us to meet a relative of hers who is due in Port Melbourne the day after tomorrow. I was supposed to go with him, but I haven't been well, you know. . . .' Kate ended her last comment cryptically, aware that it was not proper to talk about such things as pregnancy, despite the fact that she and John were delighted with the prospect of their third child. 'I'll call him, if you like. I'm sure he's not so busy that he won't have a few minutes for a friend.'

Colin nodded in gratitude, and waited somewhat nervously. He was not altogether certain how he should voice his thoughts.

'How are you, Col?' John came into the parlour, a ready smile on his face at seeing his young protégé.

Colin answered the greeting, though a little stiffly. Suddenly, he felt ridiculous about the things he wanted to say. Despite what had motivated his visit, he now found himself at a loss to explain.

'Would you like to sit down for a while?' John asked the question, sensing Colin's apprehension. 'Perhaps Kate can order some tea for you.'

'No! No, thank you.' Colin was quick to reject the offer. 'I'm not really sure what it is I want,' he went on. 'Perhaps, if I could just talk to you about some things.'

'Of course,' John agreed. He pointed to one of the leather seats, and sat down opposite. He smiled to himself as he saw Kate discreetly leave the room. John knew his wife was sensitive to the situation, and had the good sense to respond accordingly.

'What's troubling you, Col?' John tried to probe gently for an explanation.

'If I knew that, I don't think I would be troubling you.' The concern that Colin felt was evident on his face. There was a pause, as John didn't quite know how to respond to such a comment, and before long Colin noticed and realised how it must have sounded. 'I'm sorry.' He expelled a sigh of frustration. 'I seem to be so mixed up in my mind lately. I've become quite difficult to get along with, as I'm sure my mother would agree if she was here.'

'What's been confusing you, Col?' John asked, waiting patiently to see which way the conversation would go.

'I wish I could explain it without sounding absolutely stupid.'

'Just tell me what you're thinking. Perhaps if you make a start, we can sort the thoughts out into some rational order.'

'I want to get married, but I don't want to get married. Does that make any sense to you?' Colin gave a look of desperate appeal to his counsellor friend.

'All right.' John pursed his lips thoughtfully. 'Maybe we should start with the reasons why. Why do you want to get married? Are you in love with someone?'

'No! Not at all!' Colin's response was quick and defensive. 'I hope my sisters haven't been spreading any gossip about.'

'I hadn't heard anything of that nature, if that is any reassurance,' John resisted the urge to smile. 'If you are not in love with any one, is it that you feel the need of having a wife to keep your house, maybe the need for children?'

'I'm sorry, John, but that is the last thing I need right now. My house barely holds the seven of us as it is, and with a mother and four sisters, the house hardly needs an extra pair of hands.'

'They would have been my thoughts,' John agreed. 'Do you have any idea what might be a reason to take a wife?'

'I guess I'm lonely. Now that does sound stupid, doesn't it?'

'No! That sounds like a fair comment.'

'But there is so much company in my house already that it is nearly driving me crazy. In fact, I know that they are all just putting up with me at the moment. I've been very short-tempered and unreasonable. And yet, I am; I'm lonely.'

'For a companion? Intimacy? Is that it?'

'I hadn't thought of those words, but yes. I guess it must be something like that. When I look at you and at Ned, I have this feeling of envy for what you have. I want a relationship like you have with your wife.'

'And the reasons you don't want to get married are . . .?'

'Ned and Lilly have been trying to match me up with his sister, Kathleen. I suppose she is a nice girl, but I don't feel anything for her at all. She reminds me so much of my own sisters that it almost annoys me. In fact, they are really annoying me at the moment. I feel so selfish saying that, but it's the truth of the matter. I don't know what to do about it.'

'Do you feel as if you don't have any space – any room you can call your own?'

Colin thought about the question for a few moments.

'Yeah! I feel bad because of the feelings I've got, not only about my sisters, but also Harry. He is always under my feet, but he isn't any use to me. He's not old enough to share the load. I must sound like a real cad, talking like that.'

'If you were saying it all around the countryside, complaining at every opportunity, yes, you would be a cad indeed, but it is perfectly acceptable for you to share your frustrations with a trusted friend. Perhaps, together, we can find a solution. That is certainly better than holding onto resentment for years, and having it eventually seep out in your attitude and behaviour to your family.'

'I think it's already seeped out. In fact it's been pouring out. I've been really awful to my family lately.'

'Then it's high time we gave some thought to finding a suitable solution to the cause of your frustration, don't you agree?'

Colin nodded, but wondered if any such solution could be found.

Colin wondered how on earth he had allowed himself to be talked into this venture. He could not recall a time when he had been any further from Green Valley than Brinsford, and yet here he was, setting out from the Brinsford station, on a train bound for the city of Melbourne. An almost overwhelming urge to flag the train down and to demand to be let off fought with his logic.

'How long has it been since you've had time away from your family and the farm?' John asked the question, oblivious to Colin's inner turmoil.

'I don't recall having ever been away, except for some overnight trips when we took stock to the market at Brinsford.' Just making this comment triggered off a series of thoughts in his mind. He knew that he had actually been born in Melbourne. His father, an Irish immigrant, had met his mother there, not long after she had arrived with her family from England. They had fallen in love, married, and then begun the long struggle to find work, eventually saving enough to purchase the small parcel of land that Colin now farmed. At that time, the land around Green Valley was cheap, because it was so far away from the city. Only Lord and Lady Wallace from the higher social order had seen any vision for the area at all. Apart from what was now the Wallace estate, the rest of the Valley had been broken up and sold off in small allotments to the hopeful free settlers. This was their big opportunity in life to make something for themselves and their families, rather than leasing a plot from some tyrannical landlord. It didn't matter to pioneers, like Colin's father, that he would literally have to pour his blood, sweat and tears into the virgin land. Charles Shore had known that he would probably never see the prosperity he hoped for. He had acknowledged that his dream would probably not become a reality until his grandchildren were born and able to work the land for themselves. Still, he had forged on in hope for their future.

'Don't worry about your family, Colin,' John's voice broke into his thoughts. 'They'll be all right.'

'Yes. I know.' Colin had fought with the guilt that insisted on accusing him of desertion from the moment that John had suggested he accompany him to Melbourne. At first, Colin had smiled wistfully at the idea of making such a trip, never considering for a moment that it would be feasible. But the good reverend had investigated the possibilities thoroughly, not leaving a single stone unturned, as it were. Every objection that Colin could think of was examined and dismissed as easily made up. The test of putting the proposition to Mrs Shore was the final confirmation. Colin's mother, far from being put out by the idea, or even feeling in the least bit inconvenienced, reassured her son that she and the girls would manage the farmyard chores perfectly well. To set his mind at ease, she promised that she would call Ned if anything major were to occur. Finally, Colin had to admit that there was nothing pressing at the moment that could not be left until next week, and so Reverend Laslett gained a companion for his journey to Melbourne.

Now, sitting in the railway carriage, Colin began to observe the contrast in the way people conducted themselves. Even his confidant and friend had taken on a completely different air from the one he normally exhibited when he helped Colin out with various jobs around the farm. Suddenly, Colin became conscious of the fact that these people were from a different class – a world where folk lived in a social order unlike the one he was used to. Even John Laslett suddenly seemed from another class.

Colin felt the age and wear of his own clothes. He had never had anything to compare them with before, and had not ever thought that the many patches and stains would be of any account, but here, in the social context of a railway car, he stood out in contrast. If he felt this bad on the journey, what would he feel like when he got to the big city?

And when it came to interacting with the other passengers and railway stewards, Colin felt awkward, especially as he saw the grace and ease with which John conducted conversation. By the time they had reached Melbourne, Colin was thoroughly intimidated.

John sensed the slump of Colin's spirits, and had noticed his embarrassment, particularly when the pair were addressed by anyone else during the journey. It didn't take the minister long to determine the cause of his friend's ill-at-ease behaviour. As soon as John realised Colin's social dilemma, he silently berated himself for being so insensitive – for not properly preparing the young farmer, and for not warning him of what he could expect. At that moment John decided he would remedy the situation, and as soon as the pair were within a relatively private setting, he began to apologise.

'I'm sorry, Colin. I should have thought about the difficulties this trip would make for you.'

Colin seemed to know exactly what the reverend was talking about, and only nodded with relief that John understood.

'I'll take you straight to a tailor's and we'll buy you some city clothes.'

'I . . . ah . . . I don't know if I should.'

'Of course you should. I'm only sorry that I didn't think of it sooner. Having been in the country so long, I'd forgotten all about the wonderful world of fashion.'

From that moment, until the travellers entered John's sister's house, an active argument took place. It wasn't that Colin didn't appreciate John's willingness to be generous; it wasn't that John didn't appreciate the fickleness of his own class, nor that he wasn't aware of the silly lengths some of them would go, just to be one up on their own neighbour. It was more just a conflict of wills. Clearly, John was the more compliant of the two, and would have retracted the offer immediately if he had not been so aware of just how uncomfortable his companion had already found the social scrutiny. In the end, because Colin could not justify such extravagance – could not find one good reason why he should own such a grand set of garments, especially considering his sisters' shabby wardrobe – John bought *himself* a new suit, just so he could have something to lend a parishioner if the need should ever arise.

It took some swallowing of pride for the fiery-tempered farmer to even agree to borrow the suit. If it had not been for the fact that John took the exact same size as he did, Colin probably would not have agreed to it.

Still, by the time Mrs Allenby greeted the travellers, no one would have guessed that Colin was wearing anything other than his normal Sunday best.

It had been a frightening experience coming ashore. It was only a large dose of common sense that managed to give Emily enough motivation to come away from her cabin. If Mrs Manley had noticed the girl's terror, she chose to make no comment. It was as if her duty was over now that they had reached the Port of Melbourne. The older woman had only to hand her charge over to Lady

Vera Wallace's representative, and she was then free to go on her way to meet her own kin.

But despite such a mammoth effort to be brave, Emily did not find the comfort she had hoped would drive her fear away. Once on the dock, she allowed her eyes to scan the crowd, certain that most of the people standing about must have been the infamous convicts she had heard so much about.

Emily longed to cling to her chaperone's hand, just as she would have if she had been only seven instead of seventeen. But Mrs Manley pressed on through the throng of people, apparently not satisfied that any of them were waiting expressly for Lady Emily Wallace.

After an hour had passed, and the dock had all but cleared of people, Mrs Manley muttered some expression of annoyance under her breath. She had expected to find a man at least, even if not accompanied by a wife, to be holding a sign that would indicate they were waiting for Emily. When no such servant materialised, she decided to take the matter to the port authorities.

Emily followed along meekly, and eventually found herself being invited to sit and wait for her escort to arrive. There was little apology about the inconvenience, just as there were few comforts provided for situations such as this, that might occasionally arise. The afternoon had merged into evening and, much to Emily's misery, she found that she was to share the night with a very disgruntled companion, and several hard benches in the waiting room were the only bed likely to be provided.

Many times during that long and uncomfortable night, Emily questioned her own heart as to the wisdom of having chosen this course in her life.

John didn't hurry particularly that morning. Colin agreed to accompany him to the docks, but neither of them expected that the ship would be in. This day, the date that Lady Wallace had advised would be the earliest possible date of arrival, would unlikely see the ship arrive at Melbourne. John explained this to Colin during their ride through the cobbled streets, on their way to the port.

'Shipping companies can never give an exact date of arrival, like a railway company can. It takes months for a crossing from England, and there are so many things that can happen to delay a ship. They always give the earliest possible date of arrival, and then it is up to friends and relatives to make regular checks until it finally does sail in. If we're lucky, she might only be a day or two late, and we can be on our way back home within the week.'

'Do you know anything about this relative of Lady Wallace's?' Colin asked, suddenly becoming curious as to whom they would be meeting at the landing pier.

'Well, to tell you the truth, I didn't get the details straight myself before we left. We are looking for a Miss Wallace, I believe, but Lady Vera had no idea what she would look like, after all these years. I'm still not certain as to whether we are waiting for a sister-in-law, an aunt or what. I don't think they could have been close, as I got the distinct impression that she was not at all happy to be having her come to stay.'

'Lady Wallace is a grim character, though, isn't she?' Colin only recited the description he had heard from other farmers in the Valley. He had never actually met the grand Lady.

'Actually, Colin, I'm of the opinion that her bark is far worse than her bite. Let us hope that her maiden aunt is not as formidable a character as she is.'

The reverend and the farmer almost turned away from the wharf and returned home when they saw that there was no sign of any ship, or of anyone expecting a ship. But John felt it best they check with the port authorities, and leave a name and address should the ship arrive in the mid afternoon. 'That way, Miss Wallace can catch a cab to my sister's, and we won't have to be waiting around the quay all day.'

Colin accompanied his friend into the office building, and stood back, waiting while John approached the clerk. He was rather taken by the sight of a pretty young girl who sat on one of the benches, obviously watchful, expecting someone. On the other side of the room, he saw an older, matronly woman, and while the look on the girl's face was one of misery, the look on the other's face was one of thunder.

'Oh, my goodness!' Colin heard John exclaim. 'It arrived yesterday?'

''Tis a rare occurrence, to be sure,' the clerk explained. 'Such smooth sailing, she got here ahead of schedule.

At that point, Colin saw the older woman stand up and approach them both. 'Are you Lady Vera Wallace's representative?' she asked, none too pleased.

'Yes, madam. I must assume you are Miss Emily Wallace, and I can only offer my sincere apologies for not being here to meet you straight off the ship.' John saw the woman's agitation, and sought to calm her by his words. 'My name is Reverend John Laslett. Lady Vera Wallace has sent us to accompany you to her home.'

It was then that it happened, and confusion broke out right across the room. Colin had been focusing on the older woman, hoping that she wasn't really as disagreeable as she looked, when he was taken completely by surprise. The girl, who had been sitting on the other side of the room, approached Colin, holding out her hand in expectation of his taking it in greeting. Colin responded, unable to refuse the offer.

'You must be my cousin,' she cried. 'Oh, you don't know how much I've needed one of my own family. It has been awful.'

Colin was dumbfounded, and looked helplessly to his counsellor for guidance.

'Lady Emily!' Mrs Manley's tone was as stern as her countenance. 'It is not proper for such forward behaviour in public, even if the young gentleman is your cousin.'

'Lady Emily? Emily Wallace?' John looked surprised, slowly readjusting the characters in his mind. It took him a moment to reconcile the lovely young girl with the title of Lady Emily Wallace. Even in the formal Melbourne society, John had rarely interacted with someone of aristocratic birth who was so young, and of course the casual society of Green Valley had only the ostentatious Lady Vera. Neither Colin nor John had expected someone as young as this, and had been looking for someone much older.

During the short moment it took for the four of them to regain their composure, Colin had found himself yielding to the openness of the affection-starved girl. He told his confused mind, as she kissed his cheek, that it was just like when he had said goodbye to his younger sisters. But in spite of this much recited justification, he had to admit that this was nothing like interacting with his sisters. This was something entirely new, although it lasted for only five seconds, maybe less.

'I beg your pardon, madam.' John struggled to regain control of the disorder. 'I was not expecting . . . that is I

assumed . . . Mr Shore, I think you had better allow yourself to be properly introduced. Miss Wallace,' he elected
to use the more accessible title of the average Australian,
and she didn't seem to mind, 'I regret to inform you that
this young man is unfortunately not your cousin but
rather Mr Shore, a neighbour of your aunt's.'

John offered a weak smile, which was the best he could
do in the face of the impropriety of the situation.
However, if he thought that making an accurate
introduction would correct the scenario, he was very
much mistaken.

Emily quickly pulled back from the stranger she had so
hoped was one of her family. A blush climbed in her
cheeks, and tears welled in her eyes. She was thoroughly
mortified that, in her desperate need to be reassured, she
had made the very worst mistake of her life. Without
saying a word, and without waiting for the censure she
was sure her guardian was about to give, she hurried out
of the waiting room, completely disregarding her earlier
fear of being attacked by a convict.

'Well, that was certainly a colourful introduction,
Colin.' John could not help his sense of humour, no
matter how hard Mrs Manley scowled at him. 'I take it,
then madam, that it is the young lady we are to accompany back to Green Valley, and not yourself?'

'I wish to be on the first train available to Geelong. My
son has his family on a property in the vicinity of that
town. I do wish you had brought your wife with you,
Reverend. Lady Emily is in sore need of a woman's
guidance, I should say.'

'It would appear that perhaps you are right,' John
agreed quietly.

CHAPTER 3

*T*he whole day and evening that followed the incident at the dock was a very tense affair. After John had properly thanked Mrs Manley, and had assisted in finding her a cab to send her on her way, he tried his best to put the two younger people at ease. But it seemed that the more he tried, the more awkward they became with each other.

On Colin's part, he was very much aware of his own lack of class and poise. He didn't notice Emily's misery so much as he noticed her polished demeanour. Despite having spent a difficult night in an unfriendly and uncomfortable waiting room, she maintained an air of elegant charm – an attribute that seemed totally regal in comparison to the women of his own family. The observation was not intended to be critical of the Wallaces nor condemning of the Shores, but it was inevitable and there was nothing that Colin could do to prevent it. Nor was there anything he could do to prevent the total sense of inadequacy that would flood his senses every time he was left to his own thoughts.

Emily's feelings during the trip back to John's sister's, and on into the evening, were mostly of an overwhelming sense of shame. She could not allow herself a moment's peace as she mentally tortured herself for her lack of discretion. It was all she could do to form polite and sensible answers for Reverend Laslett and his sister, Mrs Allenby. Somewhere, reaching into her foggy world of self-recrimination, she was conscious that her new chaperone and hostess were trying their very best to make her feel at ease and welcome. There were moments when she almost let go of the humiliation, and nearly allowed herself to accept their attempts at friendliness; but it only took another glance at Mr Shore for Emily to return to her anguish. His silence and stern expression born of his own insecurity, appeared to her as that of a man disapproving and offended. One glance and all the mortification returned to shame her.

'I hate to sound rude, brother dear,' Sandra confided, once her house guests had been shown to their respective rooms for the night, 'but I don't think I could have stood another minute of that . . . what was that?'

John had to laugh. For him, it was a release of nervous tension in itself. Now that it was too late to make other arrangements, he had to admit that having brought Colin along must have been the worst possible choice of travelling companion, and he began to share the whole tangled dilemma with his sister.

'So, you can see that with the one so totally embarrassed with her behaviour, and the other so thoroughly intimidated by her social grace, I have made a very poor job of introductions, haven't I?'

Sandra had to laugh along with her brother. It helped lighten the load. 'Thank goodness that Leonard is away on business,' Sandra said. 'That would have been the final straw – my husband and his insistence that etiquette and social order must be observed. With your dusty farmer and his lack of confidence, and the impulsive young lady who won't forgive herself, what a dinner party they made up!'

'The poor child.' John eventually made the observation, as he returned to a more serious frame of mind. 'Fancy coming all this way to a strange land, not knowing anyone, and being so hopelessly disappointed.

She was so desperate to find someone she could lay claim to as family.'

'Poor Mr Shore!' Sandra threw in. 'He must have been thrown in the deep end. I'm surprised he is so well dressed, after all of Lady Wallace's raving about the riff-raff of the Valley. To hear her speak of the farmers, one would have thought they were a step up from a street sweeper.'

'Now you're showing your social prejudice, Sandra,' John growled. 'Just you remember all the trouble we went through when Kate and I were married.'

'Yes, I know. Those were hard times, John, and Kate suffered so much. But really, I think Lady Wallace must exaggerate the state of the small landowners. Your Mr Shore dresses very nicely, and looks quite presentable.'

'You'll have to forgive me,' John lowered his voice. 'Mr Shore is currently borrowing one of my new suits. He is like everyone else in the Valley: unable to afford any clothes that would be good enough to be seen in the church, and far too proud to accept charity. You know that I have two congregations, Sandra. There are those that Lady Wallace approves of, and who dress according to her standard. They meet every Sunday in the church. The other congregation includes folk like Colin Shore. Lady Wallace sees them as pests who will soon lose what little they do own. She is willing to wait until they fail, and then she hopes to buy up their smallholdings. In the meantime, she applies as much pressure as she can to them, and one of the ways she does this is to make sure that a class separation is observed. It's a nasty business, Sandra, and it has been a hard job for Kate and me to remain neutral.'

'So, your young farmer wears a borrowed suit.' Sandra sounded thoughtful. 'Wouldn't that be a poke in the eye for the high and mighty Lady Wallace, to find that her titled niece has been keeping company with one of such low descent.'

'Apart from that ill-timed exchange, Mr Shore and Miss Wallace have hardly so much as looked at each other. I think that Lady Wallace's social order is quite safe.'

Colin swallowed the lump of anxiety that would form in his throat every time he determined that he would act positively. Before the party of three had left the Allenby house and embarked on their journey back to Green Valley, Sandra Allenby had taken Colin aside to give him some friendly advice. Colin had not been able to formulate any response whatsoever to his hostess's words of wisdom. He was so thoroughly convinced that he was well outside of his own realm, and that he was anything but able, that he was quite powerless to even disagree with Mrs Allenby's suggestion. Of course, she had been quite gentle and sweet in her approach to him, quietly describing the feelings of the young visitor – how the young Lady Wallace was so ashamed and embarrassed of her behaviour, that she was afraid that Mr Shore would never forget the incident, and she was most certain that he would never forgive. On one point, the young farmer could agree. He was certainly unlikely to ever forget the feeling of holding her delicate hand, or the feeling of her lips brushing against his cheek as she'd kissed him. As to forgiving her, he guessed that if all the facts of his position in society had been laid out correctly, that he would be the one in the seat of guilt and consequently in need of forgiveness. But Colin had not found any words to describe these thoughts to the gracious lady of Allenby House. He had merely nodded, and breathed a sigh of relief when she had finally finished instructing him on the best possible course for reconciliation.

Now, as he sat opposite the unhappy young lady, Colin recalled what Mrs Allenby had advised. He remembered now that she had all but begged that he relieve the young lady's mental anguish by involving himself in an open and friendly conversation with her. The well meaning hostess had felt that such an act would eventually set the girl's mind at ease, and that she would soon forget her own moment of foolishness. 'Apply a little of that charm you gentlemen seem to be so adept at using when you want your own way.' Colin felt himself blushing as he remembered the older woman's words. 'No lady will be able to resist a handsome face like yours,' she had added, archly.

Yet here he was, stuck in a train carriage for at least another three hours, the urging words of Sandra Allenby playing over and over in his mind, but utterly unable to voice any sensible thought. He wondered if he might not ignore the commission for just a few more hours until he parted company with the reverend and his charge. After all, if Miss Wallace had thought him unwilling to forgive an indiscretion, or even if she had thought him rude, what did it really matter in the long run when she found out that he was of such low breeding that he was only worth her disdain anyway? That was Lady Vera Wallace's reputation in relation to the poorer families of Green Valley, and Colin had no doubt that the niece would hold to the same arrogant opinion, once she knew the truth.

But something in the mournful look, the miserable expression, and sadness that hung over Emily Wallace tore at Colin's heart. It was not that he had sat there

Green Valley

staring at her, no matter how much he was tempted, but he had chanced a number of quick glances, and his eyes told him that she was absolutely lost and homesick, not to mention mortified at having disgraced herself.

Eventually, some two and a half hours into the train journey, Colin resolved that he would follow the advice offered him.

'Miss Wallace.' The first words came out rough and throaty, and startled both the young lady and the reverend. John was in fact most surprised that his friend had addressed the girl at all, as he had resigned himself to the fact that the two younger people would probably never communicate again in their entire life.

'I hope you won't find our country too hard for you,' Colin began. 'I can't imagine what it would be like to be so far away from my home.'

At first Colin thought that she would not respond. Her face remained set in despair, and she seemed very pale, but as he made a concerted effort to maintain eye contact, instead of yielding to the urge to retreat back into himself, Emily Wallace finally allowed herself to reply.

'I never thought I could feel so alone, Mr Shore.' She spoke in a small, almost frail voice. 'It's as if every single thing that has been familiar to me is nowhere within my reach. Sometimes I think I must panic. There is nothing secure that I can hold on to. I suppose that's why . . . . '

She broke off short, but both men guessed what it had been she was going to say.

'You mustn't be so hard on yourself, Miss Wallace,' Colin spoke kindly. 'I'm not the kind of fellow who's going to think badly of you because you needed some reassurance. I'd kiss you myself if I thought it would make you feel any better.' Colin's heart of compassion was obvious, even if his expression was somewhat clumsy.

John saw Colin's lack of propriety, but didn't blame him for it, considering the kind of casual life he led as a farmer. Instead, John gave a smile he hoped would ease any tension. Colin saw the smile, and misinterpreted John's motives. He was irritated at his friend's apparent lack of feeling, and would have spoken his thoughts if Emily had not joined in with a smile of her own.

'This is a different country, and I suppose that there must be different ways of conducting yourself from the etiquette I've been taught. I do hope my brother and father never hear of my . . . what should I call it?'

'Don't worry any more about it, Miss Wallace,' John reassured. 'Let's agree, all three of us, to put that incident behind us, and we can start from the beginning again.'

John's tone and spirit was infectious, and soon brought confidence back to the normally vivacious personality of Emily Wallace.

'Miss Wallace,' John went on in a dramatic manner. 'May I have the privilege of introducing you to one of your new neighbours, and a very good friend of mine, Mr Colin Shore. Mr Shore, Miss Wallace.'

'Colin?' Emily suddenly came alive with interest. 'Have you Irish ancestors?'

'My father was Irish,' Colin admitted quietly, not as easily able to put aside his own reserve.

'My word!' Emily sounded scandalised. 'There are not many pleasant things said about the Irish in my part of the world. I don't mean any disrespect, sir,' she hurried on, not wanting to offend. 'I have never actually met an Irishman before. From the tales I've been told I'd have imagined someone far uglier and meaner. But perhaps your mother is English?'

Colin was tempted to take offence at the obvious prejudice, but he couldn't detect any unkindness in her words – only narrow-mindedness, which he was willing to blame on her upbringing.

'Perhaps you had better not taunt the poor fellow about his ancestry,' John coached, himself now in a teasing frame of mind. 'For all we know, he may turn very mean and ugly come the full moon, and it would pay for us to be on his good side then.'

Colin glared at his friend. He was finding the transition from serious compassion to light-hearted frivolity rather difficult.

Emily noticed, and was instantly repentant. 'I'm sorry, Mr Shore,' she apologised. 'Here, you have just forgiven me for my first offence, and I've immediately committed a second. My father has always said that I am far too opinionated. You must not blame him for my mindless babbling.'

Colin was not so quick at formulating a response in any conversation, and so he remained silent.

'Tell me about your family, Mr Shore,' Emily commanded. 'Are you married? No! Of course not! You are too young!' She answered her own question quickly. 'Do you have sisters or brothers, perhaps?'

'I have four sisters, in fact, and one brother, Harry.'

'Four sisters!' Emily cried, delighted at the prospect. 'Do you still live with your parents, then, and your sisters?'

'My father was killed in an accident, several years ago. We all live with our mother on the land he left us.'

'I'm sorry.' Emily showed her sympathy for one thoughtful moment, but soon moved on to her next thought. 'And you are close neighbours with my Aunt Vera? I shall be able to visit with your sisters often then? Are any of them my age?'

Colin looked helplessly to John, who had made himself comfortable observing the exchange.

'I . . . ah . . . .'

'It isn't polite to ask a lady's age,' John came to the rescue, 'but I would guess that Julianne and Christine would both be near you in years.'

'And neither of them married?' Emily's excitement increased as she imagined the new friends she would be able to meet.

'My sister, Julianne is engaged to a friend of mine. They have not set a wedding date yet, but I'm hoping it won't be too long.'

'Oh, I hope I shall have a chance to meet her, and your other sisters too. Perhaps my Aunt Vera will hold a ball for me, when I arrive. That way I could meet your whole family, and the other young people of your acquaintance.'

Colin was about to open his mouth to inform her of the truth of the situation, but he saw John caution him. He wondered why his minister friend didn't want to let the young lady know that they were merely farmers, scratching out an existence on a small piece of land that was hardly able to support the seven of them. He didn't understand John's methods at all. The very idea of Lady Wallace holding a ball at all was almost enough to make him laugh, but to think that he and his sisters could actually be invited to such an unlikely event was stepping into the ridiculous. Still, that was the idea that young Emily Wallace had fixed in her head, and John didn't seem inclined to shatter her planning, at least not for the moment. Colin's face of disapproval must have told John all he needed to know, and it wasn't too long before the minister decided he had better correct some misconceptions.

'I'm sure that all of Mr Shore's sisters would be delighted to meet you, Miss Wallace,' John spoke openly, 'however, I think I had better warn you that your aunt is not particularly inclined towards entertaining guests. I have never known her to throw a ball, or even a large party. She keeps pretty much to her own company.'

'Oh.' Emily's disappointed was clearly written on her fallen features.

'You will indeed find the Australian people different from those you have associated with back in England, but I'm sure that you will meet a number of fine young people, just like Mr Shore, and that you will learn many new things in this different culture.'

Colin was not satisfied with John's explanation, but he didn't feel he should contradict him openly. He held his peace for the rest of the journey, but he determined that he would speak to the reverend about this funding of a false notion the moment he had a private opportunity.

By the time Lady Vera's private carriage, carrying the three travellers from Melbourne, approached Green Valley, Colin found his mind and emotions in a whirl of confusion. It had only taken the offering of his forgiveness and friendship for Emily Wallace to break from her shell of depression into her normal bubbly, chatty manner. Of course, Colin was not aware that this liveliness was only heightened by the fact that Emily was in awe of what she believed to be a handsome, well mannered gentleman.

Colin wondered if he may not have slipped into the role of a hypocrite as he recalled his most recent attitude towards his sisters' giggling and chattering. He knew that Julianne's mooning and sighing about her beau nearly drove him to distraction, and of course, Christine and Samantha had offered plenty of opinion and encouragement when the subject was romance. The only way Colin had been able to avoid what he considered feminine nonsense was to go outside; in the dark on his own.

Now, as he had already endured hours of pointless small talk and lively discussion on every social issue imaginable, Colin was finding it very hard to resurrect that same feeling of annoyance. The closer he got to home, the more he felt obliged to judge the conversation in the same way he always did for his sisters. But he had reached the point of admitting that he found Emily's clear and cheerful tone as desirable as the air he breathed – never mind that fact that he understood little of the intricacies of English society.

'Thank goodness that is over.' Colin breathed a profound sigh of relief as soon as he alighted from the vehicle.

'What? Thank goodness what is over?' John was taken aback by the comment.

'Never mind!' Colin was aware that Emily was still inside, waiting for the reverend to get back in, after bidding his friend goodbye. 'Thank you for taking me on this trip,' he added. 'It has certainly been an eye-opening experience, if nothing else.'

'I hope that the time away has helped you put some of your thoughts in order,' John offered. 'Perhaps you will see things at home differently from now on.'

'Perhaps.' Colin didn't sound hopeful.

'Are you sure that you wouldn't like to come all the way with us. Hodges would be happy to drive you home after we deliver Miss Wallace to her aunt.'

Colin shook his head in the negative. 'I've only two miles' walk from the road here. It won't take me more than half an hour, if that.'

'I know, but Miss Wallace is a little upset at us just leaving you, apparently in the middle of nowhere.'

'Which reminds me,' Colin took the thought up. 'I do wish you would explain my situation to her in clear terms. She should understand just how different a situation like mine is from hers. I don't think she will ever meet my sisters, as she has shown so much wish to.'

'I don't see any reason why she should not meet your family, Colin. Your mother and sisters are fine, Christian women.'

'Don't make me argue with you about this, John.' Colin was frustrated with his friend's attitude. 'You know as well as I do that Lady Wallace would not tolerate the idea for a moment. It is wrong for us to give Miss Wallace a false impression and hope.'

'We shall see. Now I must continue on. It has been a long journey, and I am sure that Miss Wallace must be very anxious to meet her aunt at last.'

Before Hodges drove the carriage off down the road, Colin allowed himself to be dragged into one last formality. John had coached him in the procedure, and he followed the instructions to the best of his ability. 'It has been a pleasure making your acquaintance,' Colin recited, taking hold of Emily's hand and bowing slightly over it as he did so.

'Thank you, Mr Shore,' she blushed in return. 'I do hope we shall see you again before too long. I am most eager to make the acquaintance of your sisters.'

Colin didn't make any reply or excuse, casting a meaningful look towards John.

'I'll look you up soon,' John promised Colin, 'just to see how you're getting along.'

'Thanks!' Colin answered, unhappy that he was taking up John's time. 'I will return your suit to you as soon as I can.'

'No hurry,' John assured. 'You may find you have more use for it yet.'

'I doubt that, sir,' Colin was firm in his reply. 'I seriously doubt that.'

CHAPTER 4

*C*olin's first sight of the dilapidated home cabin, since being away, aroused a strange sense of ambivalence. It was almost dark by the time he arrived, but he could easily make out the farmyard, with the many fences he had built with his own hands, and the small mud and timber house his father had built when the Shore family had settled there some seventeen years ago. His first sensations were of familiarity and an impression of security, knowing that he was once again within the bounds of his own domain. Here he knew what was expected, and what it was that he was responsible for. At this small and seemingly insignificant farm, Colin held a place of authority and leadership. He provided and cared for his mother and siblings, and they loved and cared for him. This was his home. But no sooner had these comforting thoughts passed through his mind than they were overtaken by a restlessness which disturbed the comfort of his homecoming. It was hard not to compare the small three-roomed dwelling with the grandeur of Allenby House. Mrs Sandra Allenby had offered Colin one of her guest rooms, which would have been just a few feet short of containing his whole home. In that one guest room, Colin had stayed alone, sleeping in a large, double bed with springs and a feather mattress. The home-made patchwork quilt that Rose Shore had pieced together out of worn out garments could not possibly compete with the satin coverlet which had covered that guest room bed. Even thinking about the difference in the two living conditions caused Colin a wave of shame. He wasn't certain whether he was ashamed of the fact that he had been living in such extravagant luxury for the last week, while his family remained in conditions of stark contrast, or whether he was just ashamed of the way he lived altogether.

Colin pulled angrily at the starched collar of the borrowed suit. *It's perfectly ridiculous to be entertaining such notions*, he recited to himself. *I have no place in the rich man's world, and they have no place in mine.* Having pronounced this reprimand to himself, Colin mounted the veranda steps, determined to shake the strange and unsettling ideas from his thoughts.

'Mama! Colin's home!' Colin heard his younger brother immediately report his presence, the moment he put foot through the door, and within moments, the whole family had turned from their duties, excitement buzzing in the welcome.

'Look at you, Col!' Christine exclaimed. 'You look . . . you almost look dashing.'

'Almost!' Colin was sensing that old annoyance again.

'Never mind almost, son,' Rose broke in. 'You do look quite handsome. What a wonderful-looking suit. Where'd you get it?'

Before Colin had the chance to explain anything, his sisters launched into a series of questions.

'Did you buy something new for us as well?' Samantha immediately demanded. 'I've never had a brand new dress before.'

'How could he afford a brand new dress for you, silly?' Christine threw her a withering glare. 'He could hardly afford a suit for himself, let alone having any money to buy something for us.'

Colin felt mortified when he understood what they must have believed. 'This is not my suit,' he quickly explained. 'Reverend Laslett lent it to me, you see.'

'Why?' June asked innocently. 'Did someone steal your clothes?'

'Never mind, girls.' Rose saw the problem that had arisen, and wanted to avoid a fight. 'I'm sure that Reverend Laslett has some very fine relatives in the city, and he wouldn't want our Colin to sit down to dinner in his working clothes, now would he.'

The girls seemed happy enough with this explanation, but were still eager to extract whatever information they could from their brother.

'Tell us, what did you see?' Julianne, though the eldest, was no less eager to hear of her brother's adventure. At first Colin was reluctant to share of his travelling experience, but his mother gave him a warning glare, and he realised that it was the least he could do, since he had not even thought to buy a present for any of them. The five younger children sat overawed by even the simple things Colin described. It seemed as if they were soaking up even the smallest, most unimportant detail that he had to offer. Just to hear of the cobbled streets, and the horse-drawn tram cars, not to mention the quayside and the seagulls, seemed to be enough to amuse the family for the entire evening. It was hard even for Rose to call the family back to the task of preparing tea, but she insisted, despite her own desire to hear of the sights and sounds of Melbourne.

'And what about this relative of Lady Wallace's?' Julianne asked after they had finished clearing up the evening meal. 'Who was it?'

'Reverend Laslett was to meet and escort Lady Wallace's niece, Miss Emily Wallace, back here to

Green Valley.' Colin was horrified to find his stomach give a lurch just at the mention of the young lady's name.

'Her niece?' Christine was all ears. 'How old is she?'

'It's impolite to ask a lady's age,' Colin recited, 'but I guess she would be about your age.'

'And I bet she is just as arrogant and rude as Lady Wallace. Can you imagine? Two of them strutting about, full of their own self-importance.'

'No!' Colin found himself jumping to Emily's defence. 'Miss Wallace was nothing like Lady Wallace. Not in the slightest.'

As he thought of her again, Colin felt the colour climbing in his cheeks and he hoped that no one had noticed, but in vain.

'Was she beautiful?' Christine prodded, fully aware of the mischief she was making.

'I do believe our Colin has fallen in love with a fine lady.' Julianne was no less malicious in her teasing.

'Was she, Col?' Harry asked innocently. 'Was the lady very beautiful?'

Colin could hardly ignore his younger brother's guileless request for information, even though he was thoroughly irritated by the two older sisters.

'Yes, Harry,' Colin caught his gaze alone, ignoring the others. 'Miss Wallace was very beautiful.'

'Was she like a princess?' Harry was totally mesmerised by the tale.

'I've never seen a princess,' Colin tried to change the subject.

'What did she wear?' Samantha asked unaware of her older siblings' teasing.

'I don't know, Sam. I don't know much about what ladies wear.'

'Just try to describe it, Col. This is important to us.' Julianne was not giving her brother a chance to escape scrutiny.

'Julianne!' Rose decided to intervene. 'You're being a little unfair to your brother.'

'He had a week away in the city, and didn't even bring us a present. The least he could do is try to describe Miss Wallace's dress for us.'

Colin sighed as he inwardly admitted the charge against him. 'Miss Wallace is very rich, Julianne,' he tried to make a vague excuse. 'She seemed to be all frills and lace.'

'Ugh!' Harry wasn't impressed.

'I wish I had seen her. I've only ever seen Lady Wallace from a distance, and she always wears some dull colour like brown or black.' Christine's analysis was not very complimentary to the lady.

'Well, Miss Wallace is nothing like her aunt, like I said. She is very young, and very pretty, and her clothes and hair are . . . I don't quite know how to describe it.'

'I hope we can find an excuse to visit the manse,' Samantha suggested. 'If we are lucky, we might catch a glimpse of Miss Wallace.'

'Don't be ridiculous, Sam,' Julianne growled. 'She wouldn't want to see anyone like us. I dare say we had better keep out of sight. We wouldn't want our brother's romantic image shattered with the sudden appearance of the poorly dressed relations.'

'That's not fair!' Colin stood to his feet, and shouted at his sister. 'I haven't tried to create any illusions at all, romantic or otherwise.'

'So she knows that you are just a poor farmer, then?' Christine was just as ruthless.

'Reverend Laslett is going to explain our situation,' Colin defended.

'Well that will be the end of it then, won't it? Once she knows who you really are, I dare say that not even a fancy suit will be enough to win her good favour!'

'Julianne, you are being cruel and unkind.' Rose made an attempt at peace.

'For your information, Miss Know-it-all, Miss Wallace has all but begged me to introduce my sisters to her. She asked me several times.' Colin was verging on angry.

'And you told her . . .?'

'What do you think? What was I supposed to tell her?' The anger bubbled over now. 'Honestly, Julianne. How could I promise her such a thing when we all know what her aunt would have to say about such an exercise?'

'So you told her?' Christine sounded just a little disappointed.

'No!' Colin felt more guilty now than ever. 'Reverend Laslett intends to explain our position to her just as soon as he thinks he can.'

Colin was totally annoyed. He loved thinking about Emily Wallace, but he resented having to share his thoughts with his prying sisters. He wished that they weren't so astute at analysing his thoughts, and turning them into ammunition to throw back at him.

'I need to return this suit to the manse soon,' Colin sought to change the subject. 'Would you be able to wash this shirt for me, Mother? And I think I would like to take some eggs and fruit over to Mrs Laslett. I don't quite know how to repay John for the opportunity he's given me.'

'Could we take the suit and eggs over?' Samantha was quick to offer.

'If you want to.' Colin tried to sound as if he didn't really care. 'It's Mum's decision anyway.'

Emily shivered with apprehension as she was ushered into the magnificent Wallace mansion. It was not the size or the magnificence of the house that intimidated her, for her own English home rivalled this one in just about every respect. It was more the thought of facing her only Australian relative, having never met or heard of her before. Reverend Laslett had graciously agreed to see her right through the introduction before leaving to return to his own home. Emily tried not to think of the desirable and handsome Mr Shore. Reverend Laslett had babbled on about the Shores not being a family that her aunt would want to associate with on a regular basis, but Emily's mind refused to accept the information. She had been quite charmed by the young gentleman's quiet, kind-hearted manner, and she somehow hoped that their paths would cross again before too long.

'Well, child,' Vera Wallace's condescending tone set a cold and unfriendly atmosphere from the start. 'What is all this nonsense your father has written to me? I must say I have hardly had time to adjust to the idea of you even coming. His letter only arrived three weeks ago.' She paused in dramatic effect, waiting for the trembling girl to offer an explanation. 'Speak up, child,' Lady Wallace barked. 'I can't think what you could be meaning, gallivanting half way round the world, when your father wants you at home. He writes that you have been acting up. What is the meaning of it?'

'Perhaps we could wait until the morning to get all the answers you require,' John broke into the older woman's tirade. 'Your niece is quite worn out, and has been very much looking forward to meeting you.' John saw the tears that brimmed in Emily's eyes, and his heart went out to her. He knew that Vera Wallace always spoke in this high-handed manner, and he knew that it was most upsetting to the uninitiated. 'Could you order some tea for the moment? That would be enough to settle the young lady's nerves, don't you think?'

'Don't you be telling me my business, sir,' Lady Wallace spoke crossly at her minister. 'I know perfectly well what it is to have made such a voyage. I only want to know why it is that she has come. Her father tells me that she has refused to marry as he has arranged. I don't think that even you would want me to encourage such rebellion. Would you, sir?'

'As I said before, there will be plenty of time in the morning to be going over the particulars of the case. For the time being, I believe Miss Emily would value a welcome from you, don't you think?'

Lady Vera sniffed disapprovingly. 'We'll see about that. I hope she hasn't come here expecting me to side with her against her father. I can't be responsible for her wild notions and outbursts.'

'Please, Aunt Vera,' Emily bravely approached this stranger who was her relative, 'I will explain everything to you tomorrow. I wish that I could have met you in better circumstances, but we will have to make the best of it for what it is.'

Lady Vera sniffed again. 'Tomorrow, then, child. But see to it that you have some explanation. I won't be party to a wild scheme, do you hear. I won't have your father, the earl, accusing me of setting you against him.'

<hr/>

Emily was tempted to fall into the pit of despair that constantly beckoned to her. In the three weeks that she had been in Green Valley, at the Wallace Estate, she had found hostility at every turn. After the first introduction, when her Aunt Vera had been so aggressive and disapproving, Emily had decided that she would heed the minister's words, and look for the good woman who often hid herself behind a false pomposity. Emily had elected to trust Reverend Laslett, and his encouragement had been her only source of comfort.

Now, as she reflected on the many confrontations and verbal attacks that she had endured from her aunt, she was almost ready to give up on finding anything other than what Vera Wallace had presented – a stern, unfriendly and unsympathetic tyrant. It seemed to the young visitor that her aunt had taken it upon herself to enforce her father's will.

'Your father, the Earl has sent you to me to try and make you see reason, child,' Lady Vera had railed. This comment had come back close on the heels of a humble request that Emily had made. Other than her aunt, Emily had not seen any person in the house, save a few staff members, and she knew that these were not people she should associate with. Though she had had little social activity in her English home, as she had not yet come out, there were a few people who came and went, with whom she made intelligent conversation from time to time. There had been several large dinner parties that Emily had been allowed to attend, and before the Earl had taken ill, there had been talk of arranging her coming out ball. But now, there was no one Emily could talk to except her Aunt Vera, and each conversation with her was proving to be a frightening experience. Emily had ventured to ask Lady Vera if she would consider having a dinner party, or even an afternoon tea, to which request Lady Vera had continued her emotional assault. 'If you wanted tea parties and balls, my girl, you would have been better to stay on with your father, marry as he wished, and you would have had just what you wanted.'

Emily didn't wish to be rude, but she was tempted, this once, to try and explain her position. 'Please, Aunt Vera,' she tried. 'You cannot understand what sort of man father wanted me to marry.'

'What's there to understand?' Vera had queried harshly. 'Your father is a sensible man, if my memory serves me correctly. There is no reason that you shouldn't trust his judgement!'

'But father doesn't even know what Lord Derickson is really like.'

'And you do?' Vera was unyielding.

'I don't wish to be disrespectful about any of them, my father or Lord Derickson, but I'm afraid of the man.'

'What is there to be afraid of, child?' Lady Vera's tone had mellowed just a fraction. 'Every girl is a little nervous about her nuptials. It's something that comes to all of us sooner or later.'

'Yes, but . . . . '

'There are no buts about it, Emily,' her aunt was firm. 'It is your duty to do as your father asks.'

Emily wanted to blurt out how the son, Frederick Derickson had tried to force himself upon her, and how the older Derickson had intimated a similar desire, but such things were not discussed in polite company, and Emily wasn't sure that she would be able to even voice the horrible words, even if she tried.

'I'm sorry,' she hung her head in defeat. 'I wish I could be good, as you and father want, but I can't.'

'Can't, or won't?'

'Father did give me a choice,' Emily suddenly remembered. 'That is why I came out here in the first place.'

'Yes, but I dare say he hoped that you would become more appreciative of the things he has designed for you.

And that is exactly why I don't intend to make your stay a happy holiday. You need to feel the consequences of your disobedience. There will be no tea parties, child!'

Emily was hurt, but she understood her aunt's motives perfectly. She could see that Lady Vera was trying to make it as difficult as possible for her, hoping that Emily would soon change her mind and return to England. But what the older woman didn't realise was that even though Emily was bored and a little lonely, she felt safe for the first time in many months. She didn't have that constant nagging fear that if she were left alone, one of the Dericksons would find her, press her with seductive suggestions, or even force her against her will if she didn't yield.

As Emily sat in her room and considered the advantages and disadvantages of both situations, she saw that to turn around and go back to England would be only to place herself back into the path of constant threat and fear. No! She would not let despair overwhelm her, despite her aunt's desperate attempts to discourage her. She felt that at least the Wallace Mansion in the Port Phillip district of Australia was a safe refuge from physical and emotional harm.

Emily triumphed in her own soul for the next few weeks. She didn't argue with Lady Vera, and controlled her temper at times when she felt she must blurt out in angry defiance. There was one particular time, following one of her aunt's regular lectures, that Emily felt compelled to express her appreciation.

'I know what a bother I have been to you, Aunt Vera,' she began in her most humble tone, 'but I want you to know how much being here has meant to me. I have felt so wonderfully free here.'

Of course, Lady Vera could not possibly have understood the context of the word 'free', and she was naturally annoyed by the information that her efforts had had the contrary effect to the one she had planned.

'Free!' she snapped. 'Don't talk nonsense, child. I have tried every way possible to make you feel uncomfortable.'

'I know,' Emily confessed. 'But knowing that you are just doing your duty to my father has been enough to make me overlook your severity. This house represents safety and peace, to me.'

'You talk utter rubbish, child,' Lady Vera retorted. 'I would have hoped that you might be ready to have me book your return passage.'

'I will never return home while the arrangements stand as they were. Father said I could rot out here with the convicts if I would not marry Lord Derickson.'

'Convicts!' Lady Vera snorted her derision. 'They legislated against transportation years ago.'

'I am perfectly happy to choose you over Lord Derickson,' Emily offered. 'You might be cross all the time, but at least I know that you don't mean me any harm.'

Lady Vera was losing the wind from her sails, so to speak, and could not think of a suitable retort.

'Of course, if you no longer wish me to stay with you, I am willing to find another family who would be willing to take me in.'

'And just who do you think would take you in out here?' The older woman's confidence returned.

'I met a young gentleman, very kind, who spoke of his mother and sisters.'

'Where did you meet a gentleman?'

'Reverend Laslett introduced us in Melbourne. He is one of your neighbours, so I understand. A Mr Colin Shore.'

'Shore!' Lady Vera was suddenly refuelled for battle. 'From here in the Valley?'

Emily nodded.

'There is a family by the name of Shore who live south-east of here. They are some of the Valley riff-raff, low-born, tenant farmers.'

'He told me he owned property,' Emily became defensive.

'They let them do that, out here,' Lady Vera scoffed. 'Any street beggar can purchase a plot of land. That doesn't make them any higher in my opinion. They are low-born, and they will remain that way.'

Emily didn't wish to contradict her aunt, but she knew that Reverend Laslett had told her of her aunt's attitude before. *But he looked decent and handsome*, Emily told herself, *and he was very kind and gentle.*

Emily's resolution to express her gratitude and not her misery seemed to be the softening agent that had worked on the heart of Vera Wallace. Not that Lady Vera was any less formidable in her presentation, but it seemed that she had resigned herself to having a permanent resident living at Wallace Hall. Bearing this in mind, and with the gradual erosion of the initial charge of duty, Lady Vera found herself agreeing to invite the minister and his wife for afternoon tea. Emily tried not to show just how excited she was at this victory. She didn't want her aunt to recall her earlier commitment to making Emily's life drudgery.

Emily, starved of social contact, and particularly with someone of her own age, took to Kate Laslett the moment they met. John had waited for this invitation for nearly two months and, despite his discreet inquiries after the church services, had almost sensed the ban on social calls that Lady Vera had imposed. He knew the lady well enough to know what her motivation must have been. So, as soon as the invitation was received, he didn't take a moment's hesitation in responding.

'I know you haven't been well, Kate,' he had excused his impetuosity, 'but I couldn't refuse, when we have been waiting for so long.'

'It's all right, love,' Kate had smiled. 'I've been feeling a little better lately, and from what you have told me of Miss Emily Wallace, I should think that she would be in sore need of some friendly companionship.'

'I knew you would understand.' John bent down to kiss his wife on the cheek. 'I'm so glad I didn't send you packing when you first wanted to leave. Wherever would I be without you?'

'Stop it!' Kate pretended to be annoyed. 'You know very well that since we have been really married, I have never wanted to be further away from you than I am right now.'

'Yes, but not when you first came to the manse as my wife. Then, I think you would have taken the first opportunity to leave, if it hadn't been for your father.'

'Would you stop digging up the past,' Kate reprimanded crossly. 'I'm here now! I love you very much, and I have given you two children to prove it.'

'Three,' John corrected mischievously.

'Two and half.'

'No! That little fellow in there is definitely a whole person.'

'How do you know it's a boy? It may be another girl, you know.'

'I don't have any more girls' names. It has to be a boy this time.'

'Well, we still have another five months or so before we find out. In the meantime, we must see what we can do to relieve Miss Wallace's isolation.'

'The poor girl was so full of excitement when she thought that she would be able to meet Colin's sisters. Lady Vera has taken a stern hand with her. I'm sure she hoped to see Emily sent back to England by now.'

'Why do you think the girl has persisted in the face of such open disapproval? One would have thought that she would have wanted to return home as soon as possible.'

'I don't know, Kate. But from what I can gather, there is something terribly wrong with the man her father has arranged for her to marry.'

'There must be, for her to choose the likes of Lady Wallace over her own home and friends.'

'Well, now we have our opportunity to lighten up her existence. Perhaps, before too long, Lady Vera may even agree to letting her visit with the Shore girls.'

Kate laughed out loud at the idea. 'That will be the day, John Laslett. For goodness sake, can you imagine what such an exercise would take? Lady Vera would have to have been visited by an angel first, at least.'

Kate may have correctly evaluated Lady Vera's attitude, but she certainly underestimated Emily's silent strength of will. Despite Emily's sweet face and manners, Kate would have been surprised to find a girl who knew how to manipulate situations every bit as well as her aunt.

The minister's wife didn't hesitate to invite the two ladies from Wallace Hall to come for afternoon tea, the same afternoon she had been introduced to the visitor from England. As Kate expected, Lady Vera made excuses, apparently not wanting to oblige any of them, especially her own niece. Kate left them with the message that they were to let her know when they felt they would be free to visit, and wondered if she would ever hear from them again.

Emily, however, once having met Mrs Laslett, was determined to cultivate the relationship, and managed to wile her aunt to the point that Lady Vera agreed that she, at least, might go alone to visit the Reverend and his wife.

The following weeks, Emily was overjoyed at having extended her boundaries to the point that she felt she was quite welcome at the manse, and that she had a friend and ally in the form of Kate Laslett.

CHAPTER 5

*T*he routine seemed to be well established. Emily would plead with her aunt to join her on a visit to the manse, and Lady Vera, in her turn would complain and protest, finally yielding to the mournful looks her niece would use upon her. Emily found her trips to the manse a welcome change to the stuffy atmosphere Lady Wallace preserved at the great house.

'Are you sure you aren't being a little unfair to your aunt?' Kate had asked her young visitor on many occasions.

'Oh, no!' Emily had assured her. 'Aunt Vera doesn't want to go to the effort just for an afternoon tea. She is much more content just to sit at home.'

Kate had wondered several times whether Emily Wallace was employing the age-old feminine art of manipulation. She wasn't being judgemental in her suspicion, as she knew that she was no stranger to the techniques herself, having tried them many times on her father, and occasionally with her dear husband. If anybody could detect such a vice, Kate knew that she should be one to recognise it, even over and above all of Emily's sweetness.

Kate greatly enjoyed the lively company of the young girl. Emily was full of laughter and chatter, and yet Kate had a strong suspicion that there was something deeper that Emily was hiding behind her frivolous façade. Each time that Kate had tried to draw information out of her about her home and family, Emily had neatly diverted the conversation to some quite unrelated topic. Kate decided to bide her time. If she proved herself a trustworthy friend, Emily would open up and share her troubles with her when the time was right.

Emily, of course, had no idea that the minister's wife was so insightful, and she had congratulated herself often at having escaped the discussion of a subject so painful to her. There were things that she was hiding; things that she wished she could forget, which haunted her night-time thoughts. She worked tirelessly to erase these thoughts and memories from her mind. It was her decision that this Australian haven would become her home. There was no room in her thoughts for any consideration of going back to her father's house, for to return was to open herself, not only to the frightening behaviour of the Dericksons, but also to the disturbing memories of the past.

Day by day, Emily spent energy on trying to win her aunt's favour. She was kind and attentive; used every ounce of self-control available, and most of all, found ways to compliment Lady Vera on her accomplishments. Gradually, Lady Vera's resolution crumbled away and, though she would never admit it, she quite began to enjoy her niece's company. It took some time, but finally, she consented to Emily's most persistent request.

'All right, child!' The older woman waved her hand in the air. 'But if you take a fall and injure yourself, you have only yourself to blame. Don't expect any sympathy from me.'

Emily stepped forward impetuously and hugged her aging aunt. 'I won't fall, Aunt Vera. I have been riding horses since I was six years old. Father always said I had a very good seat and could handle just about any of his animals.'

'Go off with you,' Vera could not hide her growing attachment much longer, and didn't want her niece to see her weakness. 'But mind, you are to have a servant along with you. I don't want you roaming the countryside and getting lost.'

Emily had found another reason to love Australia. Though Lady Vera never rode anymore, she was still adamant about the necessity of keeping a good stable. It was one of those matters of pride that she simply couldn't let go of, and so Emily found several horses that were suitable for her to ride.

On previous visits Hodges, the gatekeeper, had driven Emily to the manse. But now that she was free to take a mount of her own, Emily badgered just about anyone near the stables to come along with her. There was a groom whose girl lived not far from the church, and he saw the advantage of accompanying the young lady on her rides, especially since she always ended up with a visit to the manse. He would leave Emily at the garden gate, and agree to return within an hour, using that time to call upon the young woman he was courting. Emily didn't mind, as she felt that the escort was superfluous in any case.

On this particular day, Emily wanted to visit with Mrs Laslett first. She told the young stable hand to take as much time as he liked, as she felt she would spend the whole afternoon on her visit. Kate had begun to talk to Emily about some spiritual principles, and Emily had found many questions she wanted to ask. But when she was greeted at the door, Emily was to find her plans completely shattered.

'I'm sorry, Miss Wallace,' Rebecca Smyth apologised. 'Reverend Laslett called Mrs Hodges in this morning, she's the midwife you know.'

'Yes, I knew,' Emily answered the young housekeeper. 'Is Mrs Laslett all right?'

'I hope so, Miss,' Rebecca said. 'Reverend Laslett was quite worried when it happened.'

'What happened?' Emily's anxiety was aroused.

'Mrs Laslett was in a lot of pain. Mrs Hodges says it was the baby, but it is many months from being due.'

'Could I see her?' Emily was very concerned, and hoped that the crisis would not turn to a tragedy.

'I'm very sorry, Miss Emily,' Rebecca apologised again. 'Mrs Hodges has decreed that I'm not to let anyone, anyone at all, in to visit. Perhaps I could send my brother up to the great house with word if anything happens.'

'Yes, thank you.' Emily turned away from the manse agitated and restless. There was no way she could simply go back to her aunt's home now, not with this worry on her mind. The dilemma was before her. She had sent the groom to visit with his fiancée, and didn't really expect him back for the entire afternoon. She probably should have sent him back to the estate, considering the fact that she would now have to set out on her own anyway.

Though Emily's grey gelding now stood tethered in the shade, she felt it was not going to be any bother to re-saddle him. She had seen it done often enough before, and she always checked the tension of the girth herself before she ever mounted. That much was easily taken care of. She also felt confident that she could easily find her way back to her aunt's estate. The only roads that crossed the one she wanted came in at a direct angle, and by the time she needed to leave the main road into the valley, she would be well able to see the main house. Still, Emily felt a little sorry that she would return without her escort. She felt confident enough, but she could just imagine the trouble he would be in if she turned up alone, and he was absent for the entire afternoon.

Considering this, and the fact that Emily felt upset over the news from the manse, she decided that she would simply ride for the whole afternoon. She needed to be away from people to think, and she hoped that she would be able to pray, just as Kate had been encouraging her to do. Kate needed her prayers now, more than ever, Emily felt.

Since she was alone, Emily wisely chose to ride along the main road back towards the Wallace estate. She hoped she didn't meet too many people along the way, as she didn't want reports getting back to her aunt about her being out alone. She would never have ridden alone back home in England, but her main fear was not of being lost, more than the danger of meeting one of the Derickson family. She had found alone by one of them once before – but that was something she didn't want to think about now.

She spurred her mount into a canter and allowed the miles to move beneath her. The autumn afternoon was pleasant and clear, and the wind rushing in her face seemed to have a purging effect on her thoughts. She saw the great house come into view, but she made no attempt to turn off at the gateway. She had already decided to keep on this road, and see just how far out of the valley she could go. The ground became steeper, and her horse slowed first to a trot, and then a walk. Both animal and rider were breathing hard from the exertion of speed, and now Emily began to enjoy the leisurely walk as they ascended out of the valley. She noticed the cleared land give way to virgin scrub, with eucalyptus trees becoming more abundant and dense. The tangy smell of the eucalyptus leaves fascinated Emily, as it had done ever since she had landed in this foreign land. The higher she went up the hill, the more the scrub closed in around her. At one point, she decided to look back from where she had come, and she could see the valley gradually disappearing behind the trees. She was not frightened by this, but rather inspired. When a rocky outcrop came into view, on what appeared to be the summit of the hill, Emily decided that it would be the perfect place to gain a magnificent view of Green Valley. The place she saw was rocky and barren, and without the obstruction of trees. She knew that her vision would not be blocked, if only she could reach it. The outcrop didn't appear to be along the road, but she could see that it was no more than a hundred feet off the beaten track, and she felt certain that she could reach it, and return to the path without any mishap.

Having turned the gelding from the road, and into the trees, Emily pushed ahead, determined to reach her goal. Only once or twice did she question the wisdom of her decision, but that was only when she would momentarily lose sight of her goal; but then, when it came back into view, Emily pushed her mount on, dodging through the trees, and trampling thick underbrush down as they went.

Whether Emily would have found her way back to the main road or not was a question that was not to be answered, however, as a small animal leaping from the bush spooked her horse, and he jumped forward, lost his footing on a loose rock and tumbled. Emily had no chance to recover her balance, and she was thrown clear of the horse as he fell. Her last thought, before she hit the ground and was knocked unconscious, was of her aunt.

She is going to be very angry with me, Emily thought; and then came blackness.

Colin had worked hard to convince his friend Ned that he would be perfectly all right continuing on alone. The pair of them were returning from an overnight trip to Brinsford, where they had taken a wagonload of livestock to market. As they were taking the last climb before descending into Green Valley, Ned had sighed in frustration at the snail's pace they were travelling. Colin knew enough about his friend to know that he was anxious to get back to his wife before nightfall, and so he offered the suggestion.

'You take one of the horses and go on ahead.'

'Are you sure,' Ned objected half-heartedly. 'That will slow you down even more with only the one horse to pull the load.'

'I know you're anxious about Lilly. It's better you get there to do the chores, with her in the condition she is.'

'But you won't get in till well after dark if I leave you with just the one horse.'

'Mum and the girls can manage without me quite well. It's better you take the opportunity to get home as quickly as possible.'

Ned had no desire to argue with his friend, and so they had pulled the wagon to a halt, unhitched Ned's horse, reharnessed Colin's horse, and parted company. Ned left, riding bareback, but he was a competent horseman, and would make much better time, even with this slight handicap.

It had been a slow climb to the top of the hill, and Colin breathed a sigh of relief as he began the descent into the valley. But he hadn't gone ten yards when he was startled by the sound of a large animal crashing through the bush. He pulled his own horse to a standstill, and waited to see what manner of beast was set to attack him.

It was a surprise at first that quickly turned to panic, as he saw the wild-eyed gelding, fully saddled, break through the bush and onto the road. Automatically, Colin leaped from his driver's seat, and sought to catch hold of the horse's bridle, with the intent of calming the frightened animal. He managed this feat with some difficulty, but even though he could sense the horse gradually settling, his own sense of agitation was being aroused. He saw the bleeding on the grey's front legs, and correctly assumed that it had fallen. He also noted the saddle, still on its back, though slightly askew.

Colin didn't know all the horses of the Valley, but he could tell that this was no common workhorse, and the fact that it wore a side-saddle was indication enough of whom the horse belonged to. The only ladies that he knew who would ride such an animal were Kate Laslett, and he was sure that John would not allow her to ride while she was with child, and Lady Vera. Colin sincerely doubted that the grand lady would sit on the back of a horse now, in her later years. That only left one other option, and Colin immediately confronted the emergency, knowing that Miss Emily Wallace had taken a fall from her horse and had possibly been crushed under its weight.

It had been nearly an hour since Colin had set out in search of Emily. He had pulled his rig off the road, unhitched his own horse, set the brake, and left the grey gelding tethered near the wagon. He had taken enough time to gather up the two or three things that he kept for emergencies. Into a large oilskin raincoat, he had rolled a storm lantern and matches, and took up the canvas water bag that usually hung on the side of the wagon. In the absence of an ordinary saddle, Colin had vaulted onto his horse's bare back and set out into the scrub, following broken branches and flattened underbrush.

Now, after an hour of searching, Colin began to despair. At first he had thought that she couldn't be hard to find, and that the little bit of daylight left would be enough. But he saw the sun set on the horizon on the far side of the valley, and he knew that he must find the girl in the next half hour, before daylight disappeared altogether.

Calling out again, Colin moved through the bush again. He had alternated his yelling out of her name, with the more piercing and farther-reaching bush call of coo-ee. *Dear Lord*, he prayed, *help me to find her*. Even the breathing of several desperate prayers like this didn't seem to help. With no answering call to break through the gathering twilight, Colin had only to assume one thing: that Emily Wallace was either unconscious, or dead. The very thought sent shivers of horror through the young searcher, and he pushed on with added fervour.

Night had completely engulfed the highwooded area, and Colin's dismay was at its height, for he had failed to find any trace of the missing rider. He swung down from the back of his horse, discouraged and fearful for the young lady. There was nothing left to do but camp for the night. The danger for himself would only increase if he tried to press on in the darkness.

He took down the rolled up raincoat, and laid it out flat. Taking the storm lantern, he lit the candle, and brought the glass cover down to protect the flame from the night breeze. A shiver ran up his spine as he realised that the temperature was about to plunge to near freezing. He had intended to be home by dark, and had not brought any warmer clothing, considering only the pleasant temperatures of the autumn days.

He knew that lighting a fire in this thick undergrowth would merely result in a bushfire. The scrub was dry from the long hot summer, and though the autumn rains had started, there was enough dry fuel in the immediate vicinity to set the whole valley alight. Colin realised he was in for a cold and uncomfortable night. But this didn't worry him as much as knowing that Emily Wallace was somewhere out in the darkness, and she probably didn't have the advantage of a light, or a coat of any kind. 'Miss Wallace, where are you?' Colin mumbled one last time.

And then he heard it. It wasn't a loud calling afar off. It was more like a weak groan of pain, and Colin could tell that it was close. 'Miss Wallace!' He called again, a little louder, in the direction he thought he'd heard the noise. 'Are you there?'

'Help! Please!'

Colin jumped up from the ground, at the sound of the low cry, holding the lantern high. He kept calling out as he moved toward the source. 'Where are you?' He knew she would have no sensible answer, but he had to hear her voice again if he were to find her in the black night.

'I can see your light,' Emily called back through the dark. 'Over here. You're getting closer.'

As the circle of Colin's lantern light finally fell upon the fallen figure of Emily Wallace, she began to cry, almost hysterically. On the one hand, Colin was relieved to see her alive and breathing, but on the other he didn't quite know what to do to remedy the situation.

'It's all right,' he soothed. 'Everything will be all right now.'

Emily lifted her tear-streaked face to her rescuer, and as she did so, the light fell on a nasty gash that was above her right eye, just below the hairline.

Colin knelt down next to her with the intention of inspecting her wounds. 'You have a bad cut on your head, Miss Wallace,' he offered, reaching out his hand to brush her hair away from the injury.

'My name is Emily,' she objected, in a childlike tone.

'Yes, I know,' Colin agreed. 'Miss Emily Wallace.'

'No! I can't remember. No! Just Emily. I don't know who you are.'

'We met at the dock, remember,' Colin prompted. 'Reverend Laslett introduced us.' He suspected that she didn't recognise him in his normal clothes, and it being half dark.

'I don't know any Reverend Laslett. I don't know who you are.'

It was then that it dawned upon Colin that the knock to her head must have affected her memory. 'Do you remember your aunt, Lady Wallace?'

'Lady Wallace?' Emily looked confused. 'That was my mother. Oh, I hope my father isn't worried about me. Do you think he knows where I am?'

Colin decided to give up any effort at intelligent conversation. The girl's brain was obviously addled, and there was no point wasting time on questions that yielded no sensible answers.

'I had better see to that cut, and we had better check to see that you haven't broken any bones.'

'I don't know how it happened,' Emily was still confused, but Colin retrieved his water bag ignoring her mindless babbling and intent upon action. The situation was difficult, Colin noted, but not impossible if he were to improvise. He didn't have anything with him that could serve as a bandage, but he knew enough about his sisters to know that a petticoat was excess material that would do just as well.

'Miss Wallace.'

'They've always called me Emily,' she objected.

'Emily,' Colin amended, not prepared to waste energy arguing. 'I need to use a strip of cloth to clean the wound on your head. Do you think you have the strength to tear me off a length of your petticoat?'

At first, Emily complied and lifted her riding skirt enough to get a hold of the white cotton garment she wore underneath. But it was soon apparent that she could not summon the strength necessary to tear a piece away. Politely and gently, Colin reached out to complete the task for her, and his superior strength made the job easy. But as the sound of the material ripping rent the night air, a strange thing happened – something that both surprised and scared the young man.

Emily's mind was somewhat scrambled, and the only memories that she could seem to focus on were those of her previous years in England. When she felt Colin's powerful hands tearing at her clothes, it was as if a horrible nightmare flashed vividly through her mind. She was back in the garden at her father's estate, with the lustful and violent Frederick Derickson pulling at her clothes and threatening her with a knife, should she struggle or scream out. But Emily had screamed, loudly and desperately just as she did now, out in the Australian bush. 'No!' Her voice broke the still night. 'Don't hurt me! Please. No!'

Colin was flabbergasted at her outburst, and not having any idea what was affecting her mind, he was momentarily struck dumb. As she tried to pull away from him, and being pulled up short by knives of pain from other injuries, Colin moved to reassure her.

'Miss Emily! Wait! Be careful!' he cautioned, holding back from helping her because of her obvious fear of being touched. 'I'm not going to hurt you. I'm here to help you.'

Emily had curled, as much as the pain would allow, into a foetal position, the screaming merging into quiet sobs, more from the agony of the memory than from any physical pain she was now suffering.

'It's all right,' Colin persevered, inching toward her, his hand outstretched as he would have done to win the trust of an unbroken horse. 'Who has hurt you, Emily?' He eventually asked, a fierce protective anger fuelling his compassion. 'Has someone touched you?'

'Are you one of his men?' Emily asked, the fear still quite evident in her tone. 'Have you come to finish what he started?'

'Whose men? Who tried to hurt you?' Colin felt sick in his stomach as he began to picture what must have happened.

'I couldn't tell my father,' Emily sobbed. 'He said that if I told anyone, he would tell them it was my fault – that I had tried to setu . . . sedr . . . . '

'Seduce?' Colin offered helpfully. Emily nodded miserably in return. 'Which man has treated you like this?' Colin's tone was building with anger.

'You won't tell my father, will you? I know he will think it is all my fault, and then he will make me marry.'

'Emily,' Colin tried again, using a softer tone, 'I won't tell your father, I promise. If you tell me who the man is, I promise that if he ever comes near you again, I will beat him to within an inch of his life.' Colin didn't stop to think of the implications of making such a promise, and neither did he care. Right at this moment, when Emily was at her most vulnerable, all he could feel was rage at the blackguard who had so violated her innocence.

Eventually, as Colin continued to reassure in soothing tones, Emily's mind began to clear, and she could see for herself that this man who held out his hand to her was not going to harm her.

'I'm sorry,' she finally breathed. 'It was a bad dream.'

'Dream, or memory?' Colin challenged. 'Do you remember such an incident ever happening to you?'

'It's not proper to talk about such things,' Emily excused herself. 'Father would demand satisfaction. They don't fight duels any more, but he would have demanded that I marry him.'

'Was this the man your father wanted you to marry, anyway?'

'No! It was his son.' Emily's face showed a sad mixture of shame and sorrow.

'His son?' Colin was confused.

'Frederick Derickson is Lord Derickson's son. He is already married, but that doesn't seem to stop him from . . . ' She broke off the thought, as it came up again.

'And Lord Derickson? Is he the one you're supposed to marry? How old is he?'

'Nearly sixty,' Emily answered. 'He has never tried to touch me, but I just know that he is like his son. He has that same violent look in his eyes. I'm so afraid of them both.'

'You don't have to be afraid of them now,' Colin volunteered.

'It will all be the same just as soon as you take me back to my home. Father insists that I must marry him.'

'But you're in Australia now, Emily. You're a long way from your father's house. Don't you remember?'

'Australia!' It was as if a light had come on in her head. 'I'm not in England any more?' She looked to Colin for confirmation.

'You came to stay with your aunt, Lady Vera Wallace.'

'I did? Yes . . . I think I remember. She is always cross and disagreeable, isn't she?'

'I don't know your aunt so well that I could make a judgement about that.'

'Do you work for my aunt?' Emily was still struggling to sort out the situation in her mind. Colin started again at the beginning of the story, and began the job of seeing to the cut as he talked. The narrative seemed to have a calming effect on the young lady, and she only flinched once or twice when Colin accidentally touched a raw nerve.

'I feel so foolish,' she spoke softly, a little later. 'I do remember some parts of that story. I recall just how embarrassed I was when I found out you were not my cousin at all. And now, look at me: I'm completely at your mercy again.'

'I beg you to trust me, Miss Emily,' Colin wanted to establish this point. 'If I had it in mind to do you any harm, I would have had plenty of opportunity by now.'

'I know!' Emily admitted. 'I was just frightened before. You won't tell anyone about that silly dream, will you?'

'It was more than a dream, wasn't it?' Colin challenged. 'I wish you would talk to Mrs Laslett about it, and I really think your aunt should know too.'

'Please don't tell her,' she pleaded. 'What would she think? I'm sure that she would believe that I had invited trouble; she is going to say that anyway, about this.'

'How did you come to be up here, all by yourself?' Colin suddenly became curious.

'It's such a long story, and you will just say it serves me right, when I've finished.'

'Well, we have the entire night, so it might be just as well to get all of the details straight now, so you can have your excuses ready for your aunt in the morning.'

'The morning?' Emily's eyes lit up with that fear again.

'Even if it were possible to find my way out of here in the dark, I would not risk trying to cover this uneven ground, and having you fall again. I'm afraid you may have broken a rib or two.'

This comment came after Colin had gently probed all of Emily's bones, including her ribs, and found that there was definitely something amiss on her right side.

'But how can I stay out here? I haven't a coat, and already I'm beginning to feel the cold.'

Colin knew what he had to do, but didn't quite know how he was going to explain it to the nervous girl. There was no safe way to light a fire, he knew that for certain. There was only the one raincoat, and though it was large, it would mean that the two young people were going to have to sit close together, making the best use of one another's body heat.

He might not have been brought up in high-class society, but even he knew that such an exercise was going against every rule of propriety that had ever been made. But he had already decided what was necessary. He could see Emily shivering, and he had to take into account the fact that she must still be suffering from shock.

There was nothing left to do but for Colin to hold her in his embrace for the entire long, cold night.

CHAPTER 6

olin woke feeling stiff and uncomfortable, and it took him a few seconds to recall the place and circumstances where he had fallen asleep. He held himself still for a few minutes reflecting on the best course to take, considering Emily Wallace was still sound asleep, nestled safely against his chest.

A quick glance at the surrounding area revealed that it had been a cold night. There was evidence that there had been a frost, though Colin knew that it would not have been as bad for them, under the cover of the gum trees, as it would have been if they had been down on the plain. He was surprised to find that instead of still being propped up against the tree, where he had finally fallen asleep late into the night, they were now both lying down at the foot of the same tree. He did not recall having changed position, and he hoped that he had not hurt Emily by doing so.

It was at that point that he began to worry. *Perhaps she had died in the night.* But just as quickly as that thought came, logic told him that she was still warm, and he could feel the gentle rhythm of her breathing against him.

And then a new thought struck him. He had been so tired the night before. It had taken hours of reassurance, explaining the dangers of hypothermia, explaining the dangers of bushfires and so forth, for Emily eventually to submit to the plan of leaning against her rescuer. Colin had been so involved with the whole procedure and the extra care not to alarm her, that he had not considered how it actually felt to be so close to such a delicate and desirable woman.

As the idea crossed his mind, he felt a bolt of terror course through him. If Emily had not been injured, he would have pushed her away from himself without delay. To acknowledge such feelings, Colin felt, was to place himself in a similar category to Frederick Derickson, and that was a place he never wanted to be. He believed a man like Derickson was the lowest form of humanity.

Without further consideration, Colin began to move, hoping to release himself from the embrace without hurting or waking his charge. Miraculously, it seemed, Emily did not stir from her slumber, and Colin took the coat off to lay over her still form. His first course of action was to wake up properly, shake all unwanted temptations from his mind, and to bridle his horse, ready for the ride out to safety.

'Miss Wallace.' Colin deliberately returned to using her formal name as he gently shook her shoulder. He wanted to put some safe distance between them before he was overcome by unwelcome emotions.

Emily stirred from her deep sleep, but would just as soon have been left alone, as wakefulness brought with it a consciousness of all the pain. Her entire body ached, not just from the stiffness of sleeping on the hard ground, but from the jarring and bruising she had sustained when she had fallen from her horse. Like Colin, Emily took several minutes to reconstruct the previous evening's events in her mind. As it all became clear in her memory, she began to panic, and without thought to her wounds, she tried to sit up in a hurry.

'Whoa!' Colin reached out to steady her. 'Take it slowly. We have plenty of time to get home now.'

Emily balanced herself, but she had nothing to say. She was overcome with shame and regret, and tears brimmed in her pretty blue eyes. She didn't want to cry any more in front of this relative stranger, but her bottom lip would not stop its quivering. Colin noticed, but no matter how much he wanted to draw her close to comfort her, he steeled himself, instead only putting his hand on her shoulder.

'Can you tend to yourself, Miss Wallace? As soon as you are ready, we must try to find our way back to my wagon, and then we can get you straight back to your aunt's house.'

Emily nodded in spite of herself, and pulled herself up with Colin's assistance.

'How do you feel?' he asked kindly.

'Every bone in my body aches,' she replied, 'and I feel a little dizzy.'

'Can you go behind the bush on your own?' Colin hated to ask, but it was a necessity that had to be seen to. They would not get back to the estate in under two hours, if it only took them that long.

'I'll try.' Emily bravely stepped away from the campsite, reaching out for every tree branch or trunk that was available to support her along the way. *If only I had a maid along*, she lamented to herself. This was one effort she was going to have to make on her own behalf. No matter how badly off she was, there was no way on this earth that she was going to have Mr Shore assist in this exercise. *Thank the Lord that I haven't broken a leg or arm*, she whispered in a prayer.

Colin rolled up the lamp and water bag, ready to strap them on his own back. He waited for Emily to return, anxiously listening for signs of life, still half scared that she would pass out or fall, further injuring her ribs. When she finally did make her way back into the clearing, she was none too steady on her feet. Colin went forward to take her arm, but as soon as he was close enough, Emily fell against him. 'I'm sorry,' she whispered. 'My head just keeps spinning and spinning.'

Considering this, Colin decided that she would not be safe alone on the horse. If she were to fall off, the slightest jar could push a cracked or broken rib into her lung. The risk was too great, and he wasn't prepared to take it. He no longer felt a need to explain his every action. It seemed that Emily had relinquished her fear and had thrown herself fully upon his good judgement.

Once again, it was no small feat getting the injured girl on the horse without further hurting her. There was a slight rise nearby, and Colin made use of it by leading the horse to the lower side, and then he carried Emily to the rise, and from there, he was able to put her across the horse with relative ease. He then swung his own leg across, and took hold of the reins around his passenger. This way, he felt he could be sure of holding Emily upright, and he would be able to prevent her from sliding off. It took some willpower, but Colin was determined to harden himself against those feelings that had assailed him earlier. *I am doing a job*, he recited to himself. *I would do the same thing for my sisters.*

The little voice in the back of his head that shouted out that he was a liar did not win over his determination. He, Colin Shore, would not submit to those instincts that had caused Emily so much pain in the past. Too much ground had been conceded already. Emily's honour was at stake, and there was nothing that would now induce Colin to take advantage in any way, shape or form. *No matter how much a man loves a woman*, he thought, *he cannot take away her dignity and self-esteem*. But no sooner had this thought been expressed in his mind than he wondered how on earth he could admit that he loved her. *What on earth is wrong with me? He asked himself.*

The sun was well on the way to its zenith by the time Colin pulled up his wagon at the front of the Wallace mansion.

'Hello, there!' He called out, surprised that a stable hand or gardener had not already come to see who was there. *Surely they have missed her*, he thought to himself.

'Will you be all right for a few minutes?' he asked Emily, suddenly reluctant to leave her alone, and wondering how he was going to manage once this close physical contact was broken.

'Aunt Vera is going to be very angry with me. What on earth am I going to tell her?'

'Let's just get you inside and I'll go for the doctor. There'll be plenty of time for explanations later.'

As Colin's feet hit the gravel driveway, a maid appeared at the doorstep.

'Oh! You've found her. Thank goodness. We've been worried sick.' Colin recognised the maid as the daughter of the Booths from the general store.

'Could you get Miss Wallace's aunt?' Colin called to her. 'She has been injured and will need attention immediately.'

'Injured! Oh, dear!' Alice Booth seemed shocked by the announcement, and unable to think or act.

'Hurry, Alice!' Colin sounded impatient. 'Where are all the servants? Shouldn't they be here to help?'

'They've all gone out. Early this morning. Lady Vera sent them out to search for her niece.' Alice was not going to be helpful, Colin could see.

'Could you get Lady Wallace? Please!' he added with forced patience.

But Alice didn't end up being the bearer of news, as Lady Vera, unable to endure the hours of waiting, found her way to the front door, where she saw for herself that her niece had been brought home.

'Well, don't just stand there, man,' she snapped. 'Bring her inside. Alice, turn the bed down at once, and send someone out for the doctor.'

'There is no one else here who could go,' Alice objected in her helpless way.

Colin was irritated by the inefficiency of the housemaid, and had already made up his mind that he would make the trip back to Brinsford to fetch the doctor. Meanwhile, he took every care as he lifted Emily from the wagon seat and carried her up the front steps of the mansion.

'I'm so very sorry,' Emily kept apologising the whole time it took to get her to her bedroom.

'It's all right, Miss Wallace,' Colin brushed her embarrassment aside. 'Just so long as you get well.'

'But all the things I said . . . . ' Her voice faltered as Colin placed her, as gently as his straining muscles would allow, upon her bed.

'That will do.' Lady Vera snapped her order to Colin as if he were one her own errant staff, and stepped around him as if he were of no consequence at all.

But instead of retreating graciously from the room, as any servant would have done, Colin waited a few moments more, not totally satisfied that all that could be done had been done.

'I don't know what to say to you, child,' Lady Vera began her remonstrance. 'What on earth possessed you to go riding without a groom?'

Emily had no courage to face the charge.

'And here you are, brought back to me by goodness knows what sort of man. What has he done to you?'

'Aunt Vera!' Emily summoned some energy for the defence. 'My injuries are all the result of a fall from my horse. I don't really remember how it happened.'

'There you see!' She seemed satisfied. 'He could have done anything to you, and you wouldn't even have known it.'

Colin, standing back and able to hear the exchange, suddenly chose to speak. 'I beg your pardon, Lady Wallace. Whatever happened out there, one thing is for sure, your niece might have died in the night if I hadn't found her.'

Vera turned around, surprised to still find him in the room. 'And how did you find her?' She was all accusation. 'Did you follow her out from here?'

'Please, Aunt Vera,' Emily called weakly. 'Mr Shore has only tried to help me.'

'I'm not about to stand here arguing about nonsense when your niece is in need of medical attention.' Colin took the matter into his own hands. 'If you don't have anyone to send to Brinsford for the doctor, I will go.'

'And what makes you think the child needs a doctor?' Vera knew she was being unreasonable, but her pride could not suffer being commanded by someone so obviously lower class.

'For your information,' Colin's voice rose in impatience and anger, 'I have felt every bone in her body, and I'd say she has broken ribs. And that's not to mention the worry there is about her head.'

'What about her head?' Lady Vera felt herself losing superiority.

'Can't you see the gash for yourself? People die from hits to the head, you know!'

'Thank you!' Vera snapped. 'You may go.'

'Would it be too much to ask to borrow one of your horses? Miss Wallace's gelding is all cut from the fall. My own horse has been travelling all morning. Do you have one that can run?'

'You'll have to see to it yourself,' the Lady brushed him away with a wave of her hand. 'All of the men are out searching for Emily.'

Colin ducked his head in a gesture of acknowledgment before backing from the room.

'And if you steal my horse, I'll have you flogged as a common thief!'

Though Colin expected to be two hours on the road to Brinsford, his trip was cut short as he met the doctor a little over an hour out of the Valley. Colin had not actually ever met the doctor before, and it was only chance that they had passed each other on the road, neither aware of the other's need. Now, as Colin was seated next to the learned gentleman in his one-horsed sulky, he breathed a prayer of thanks that Doctor Michaels had waved him down to ask directions.

'Thank goodness my impatience got the better of me, lad,' the rotund doctor spoke loudly. 'I would have driven right by, except I had already decided that I would flag down the next traveller to ask how much farther.'

'And I nearly didn't stop,' Colin confessed. 'I am too worried about Miss Wallace's condition. When I saw your hand, I was just short of cussing. Thank goodness my mother taught me some manners.'

'Yes, indeed!' Doctor Michaels agreed. 'Unfortunately, I will have to ride right to the manse, you know. The situation is critical, I understand.'

'The manse!' Colin was shocked by the information. 'Who is ill?'

'I'm sorry, young man. A doctor has ethics which prevents me now from telling you.'

'Yes, but Reverend Laslett and his wife are close friends of mine.' Colin's tone rose in panic. 'Is it Mrs Laslett? Is it the baby?'

'I don't know the extent of it yet, lad,' the doctor tried to get out of it. 'If they're friends of yours, I dare say you'll inquire the moment we get there.'

'But what about Miss Wallace?'

'From what you've told me, I think she will hold for an hour or two longer. If we part company at the Wallace Estate, I'll give you a list of symptoms we need to worry about. Go back and check on the girl, and if she seems in any danger, I'll come as soon as I can.'

As much as Colin was full of anxiety on Emily's account, he now had his friends, John and Kate, to be concerned for as well. What could have happened at the manse to make the doctor's presence so necessary?

Little else was said for the remaining miles into the Valley. When they drew near the Wallace estate, Doctor Michaels began to recite several symptoms that might be cause for alarm in Emily's case. He described carefully what Colin was to look for.

'Just as soon as you have examined the patient, come right on to the manse.' He spoke to Colin as if he were one of his medical colleagues. They parted company after Colin had untied his horse – the borrowed bay mare from the Wallace stables – from behind the sulky.

'Pray for your friends, lad,' the doctor shouted out as a parting word. 'Pray that the day yields no serious results.'

These words only served as a reminder of just what or just whose lives were at stake.

'Well! Where is the doctor?' Lady Vera had regained her superior air, and wielded her words like a sword, the moment Colin set foot back in the entrance hall. 'You have not had enough time to have gone all the way to Brinsford. What game are you playing at, anyway?'

'I met the doctor on the road here,' Colin explained, while fighting down the urge to explode. 'He had been called to an emergency at the manse.'

'Never mind that,' Lady Vera snapped. 'Why didn't he stop in here on the way?'

'I described Miss Wallace's condition to him, and he decided that the situation at the manse was more serious. He has sent me to check on her.'

'Don't be impertinent, boy. As if I would allow such a thing.'

'He has given me a list of symptoms that we need to look out for, and I'm to report to him just as soon as I've seen her.'

'Give me the list,' Lady Vera demanded. 'I'll have her maid check on her.'

'Alice would not be capable.' Colin's impatience was rising.

'I'll thank you to hand me the list, and kindly let me be the judge of what is best.'

'I don't have a list. Well, not a written list. It's up here.' He indicated, by pointing to his head.

'Well, if what you tell me is the truth, you had better tell me what you know right away. I'll not have my niece further intimidated by your uncouth presence.'

The temptation to brush straight past the domineering woman was almost overwhelming, especially when he considered that there were still no male servants on the property. But his good sense told him to give her the doctor's instructions.

'Doctor Michaels must know if Miss Wallace is overly sleepy and cannot be awakened; if she is nauseous, or if she develops a fever. I think those were the main concerns.'

'Think? Shouldn't you remember?'

'I'm sorry to be a bother to you, Lady Wallace,' Colin allowed a sarcastic remark. 'Perhaps if you will check for any of these symptoms, then I will get out of your way.'

Colin walked smartly out of the Wallace Mansion in an uncharacteristic display of protest. He was insulted and offended at the treatment he had been given. It wasn't that he'd expected to be hailed as a hero, but he certainly hadn't anticipated being almost accused of some criminal offence.

He returned the bay to the stables, and saw to the harnessing of his own animal to the wagon. When he had finished, he marched, somewhat annoyed, back into the house.

'Lady Vera says that Miss Emily shows no cause for alarm.' Alice relayed the message to Colin, revealing just an edge of haughtiness at occupying a higher position on the estate than he did.

'Thank you.' Colin was not satisfied at all. He felt it was his responsibility to see to Emily himself. He wanted to know that she had been thoroughly checked, and that every possible care had been taken. But as he drove his wagon away, he had to acknowledge that it wasn't really his responsibility at all. Not in real terms at least, despite the strange mix of emotions that seemed to be clouding his mind.

The further he drove away from the Wallace estate, the more Colin tried to put his thoughts back into perspective. He knew that he should be riding straight to his own home. His mother was most likely beside herself with worry by now, and yet Colin's heart seemed still to be with Emily Wallace. He could still feel the fierce sense of protection that had motivated him the whole time that he had held the young lady close. And now that he was forced to drive away from her, he felt a sickening twist of worry in the pit of his stomach. It both angered and surprised him.

Some twenty minutes later, Colin came in view of the manse. Despite his current confusion, a new fear rose up to dominate his thinking. He uttered a few lines of prayer for the wellbeing of the Laslett family, and hoped upon hope that the doctor had not been too late for whatever crisis had occurred.

As he pulled his wagon up outside the garden gate, Colin saw Doctor Michaels coming out of the front door of the manse.

He was alone, and Colin hoped that this was a positive sign.

'How are they?' he asked without further hesitation. 'Is everyone all right?'

'Can't do any more here.' The doctor shook his head sadly. 'It happens sometimes. It's just one of those tragedies of life.'

'Tragedy?' Colin was instantly afraid of what he was about to find out. 'Who? What happened?'

'I can't do any thing else here, lad. What about your young lady? How does she appear?'

Colin was now torn between the two. 'Lady Vera wouldn't let me see her. I passed your instructions on, and they told me that she was all right. But I would just as soon you go and take a look for yourself. I'm certain that her ribs are broken.'

'I'll drop in, lad. Don't concern yourself on that score. Your young lady will be fine, by the sounds of it, even with cracked ribs. Better than they've fared here, I'd say.'

Colin bid the doctor goodbye, anxious to find out what sorrow lay behind the doors of the manse.

CHAPTER 7

C Colin's heart was hammering with fear as he lifted his hand to the brass doorknocker. It was quite apparent that something had gone dreadfully wrong from the doctor's veiled report, and now was the moment of truth. There were moments when Colin felt sure he would run and hide as the memories of his father's tragic accident came to the forefront of his mind. He hated that feeling of loss, but as much as it threatened his peace of mind, he simply had to know what had taken place within the manse.

'Colin!' Rebecca Smyth spoke his name quietly, her eyes red and her cheeks tear-stained. 'It's a sad day for us here.'

'What's happened, Rebecca?' Colin's throat had already constricted with emotion.

'I'll get the reverend. He'll want to tell you.'

That information may have been a relief, but Colin had never seriously suspected that John was in danger.

John appeared in the hallway, his shoulders drooped in a distinctly resigned way. He did not offer a word of greeting, and the few words he did speak were rough and full of emotion. 'Walk with me for a while, will you Col?'

Colin was glad there was something he could do and patiently followed his friend outside, gradually down the path and to the road. His own mind was full of questions, but he didn't have the courage to ask, and so he just walked silently with the heart-broken minister for some distance.

'It was a boy.' John finally offered this information. 'I had been hoping for a boy.'

Colin waited. He couldn't find the right words to form questions.

'It was far too early for him to come,' John continued. 'We all knew it, but still we hoped that he might have held on. He did for an hour or so, but he was too small.'

At these words, John stopped and broke inside. Colin was close enough and so reached out a hand to his shoulder as a sign of support, but John took more – he needed more. He turned and clung to Colin as if he was a raft to hang onto in a raging sea of anguish.

This was an entirely new experience for Colin, acting in the role of support. He felt the racking sobs of his friend, and for a moment was embarrassed for him, but then he remembered a similar situation some six years earlier.

It's all right to cry, the words echoed in is mind. *Even Jesus cried on occasion. No one would expect you to pretend it didn't hurt.* Colin remembered how he had felt, crushed under the weight of unexpressed grief, and how much release he had experienced when his friend, this man now crying on his shoulder, had encouraged him to cry.

'I'm sorry, John,' Colin pushed the words out.

The storm seemed to subside at this point, and John straightened himself.

'You don't know how it can twist a man's stomach to see his own flesh and blood dying like that.'

'Kate?' Colin asked, suddenly afraid for her.

'The doctor says she will recover, as she has done before, but losing the baby will hurt. Col, it frustrates me so much not being able to do anything to protect the one I love from hurt like that. I don't think you could ever understand.'

'I understand,' Colin replied softly, suddenly recalling his own frustration at hearing Emily's fear, and the twist in his own stomach when he'd been forced to leave her side.

John turned back his gaze from staring out into the hills, and looked closely at the young farmer. 'I keep forgetting how you lost your father, Col. I'm sorry. I guess you understood this feeling before I did.'

'No! Actually, I've just learned all about the pain of love today.'

John's thoughts were briefly distracted from his own trauma, and he turned a questioning eye towards Colin.

'I've finally found a woman I love,' Colin confessed, 'and her hurt and pain has almost torn me apart.'

'Miss Wallace?' John guessed tentatively.

Colin nodded his head. 'It's ironic, isn't it? Of all the women in the world for me to fall for, it had to be one that I could never have.'

'You've made the right decision,' John spoke quietly, some thoughtful moments later. 'Lady Wallace would never allow such a match to take place. It is better that you leave it as it is.'

Colin sighed, disappointed that John hadn't insisted he fight the odds, yet knowing that a fight could yield nothing but more heartache and pain.

'I'd better get along home. I'm sorry to hear about your loss, John, I really am.' Colin shook his hand firmly. 'If there is anything my mother or sisters can do for your wife, please let me know. I will come by later, if you want a hand to . . . you know, a coffin.'

John fought the tears back this time. He hadn't thought about the practical aspects of losing a child, even one so tiny. 'I'd appreciate that, Col. I really would.'

Emily winced yet again as Doctor Michaels wrapped the long white bandage around her ribs.

'It is a good thing your young man took such care bringing you back,' the doctor commented. 'These ribs are broken all right, and one bump in the wrong direction could have been serious indeed.'

Emily felt a bolt of exhilaration shoot through her. It wasn't so much the confirmation that Mr Shore's diagnosis and precautions had been correct, more than the reference to him, by the doctor, as being 'your young man'.

She cast a glance in her aunt's direction, hoping that she would detect approval, instead of the general displeasure that had been exhibited ever since she had arrived back home earlier in the day. But Lady Vera showed no such expression. She had heard the doctor's comments, but was determined not to allow the rough young farmer any grace at all. She was totally incensed that her niece should have been put in such a position of compromise, and she was quite willing to blame Mr Shore for it.

Emily, however, had begun to entertain ideas that almost contradicted her aunt's. Sometime during the previous long, cold night, Emily felt as if she had fallen in love with Mr Shore. There was no logic attached to this mental admission – only the whirling emotions of a young woman who had been captivated by the actions of a strong and capable young man. Any girl would have felt the same way, given the circumstances.

It certainly wasn't Colin's rugged good looks, for she had been approached by handsome men before. Frederick Derickson was as fine-looking a man as one would ever hope to meet. Nor was it Colin's dress or deportment. Admittedly, Emily had seen Mr Shore dressed in an expensive suit, and now she had seen him looking much like the tenant farmers from her father's estate. No. The way Emily felt had nothing to do with the way Colin looked or how he dressed. Emily was totally smitten by the actions of a hero. To her, Mr Shore had been kind and gentle. He had been honest, especially at a time when he could easily have taken advantage of her, yet he had held her honour in high esteem. He had asked Emily to trust him, and in return he had treasured that trust, rewarding it with the utmost care. Emily drew in another breath and let out a dreamy sigh. There was nothing to be gained by pointing out these wonderful characteristics. Emily could tell that her aunt was too furious about the whole situation, and especially Mr Shore, to even tolerate a recital of just how wonderful she thought he was.

'Well, Miss Wallace.' The doctor appeared to be preparing for a summary. 'You are very lucky to be alive. One night, unprotected in that cold, could well have been the end of you. Still, you had God watching out for you, and thank the Lord that he sent someone as responsible as Mr Shore to your aid. I don't want you out of that bed for at least a week, and certainly not until those headaches stop. And if there is any more dizziness, you are to stay right where you are. I will need to call back to the manse next week, I should say, so I will call in on you then.'

'The manse?' Emily was surprised to hear it. She hadn't known that the doctor had been in the Valley for any other purpose other than her own need.

'Not now, child,' Lady Vera stepped forward. 'You lie back as the doctor told you, and I will see him to the door.'

'But is everything all right with the Lasletts? I had meant to visit Mrs Laslett yesterday, but her housekeeper sent me away. She had said that Reverend Laslett was worried about her. Have you any news?'

'We'll discuss it later, Emily.' Lady Vera was determined in her answer and turned to escort the physician from the room.

'You will hear soon enough,' Doctor Michaels murmured to the lady of the house. 'It would be best not to upset the girl.'

'I agree!' Lady Vera answered.

'Yes, but you don't intend to tell her what has happened. I would wager my horse that she will not rest until she has found out. I advise you tell her the truth immediately. She will have time to grieve while she recovers.'

'Grieve?' A chill stole over even the hard heart of Lady Wallace.

'They have lost the baby,' the doctor broke his confidence. 'I have only mentioned it because your niece is obviously one of those strong-willed girls who will put her own health at risk if she believes it is for a friend.'

'Yes, well thank you for your advice.' Lady Vera wanted to close the conversation quickly. She was not an expert at friendships or at dealing with troubled emotions. Her best advice in a situation like this was to just forget there had ever been talk of a baby. That would be the best cure, in her opinion.

Several weeks had passed since that fateful autumn day. The family at the manse had weathered the most sorrowful period, and John had made a concerted effort to play with his two daughters. Elizabeth was nearly six and her sister, Annie was just three years old. Elizabeth was conscious that her parents were upset, but no one had told either of the children about the baby, and so they didn't miss him one way or the other. Kate recognised this fact, and knew that she would have to haul herself back to action, despite the terrible emptiness inside. Unlike when her father had died, no one from the community came to offer condolences, other than Colin and his family. It seemed that there was some unspoken agreement that because the baby had never actually lived a life, it was as if there had been no baby at all. Kate knew differently. The tiny, undersized infant had definitely been her son. She knew that John had held an informal funeral service for him, attended only by Colin Shore and himself. Kate had already decided that the baby would have a grave marker, clearly stating his name and relationship to their family. Before he had been born, they had already settled upon the name of Carlton, after Kate's father, and Carlton John Laslett would be the name that would eventually be carved to mark his resting place.

Kate was aroused from her deep thoughts at the sound of her housekeeper answering the front door.

'Excuse me,' Rebecca spoke politely to the mistress of the house. 'Mr Shore is at the door inquiring after the family.'

'Have him come inside, Rebecca,' Kate instructed, 'and then go across to the church office and fetch my husband.'

'Are you sure you're feeling up to it?' Rebecca felt confident enough in her position to ask the question. Mrs Laslett had always shown her friendship as an equal, and now in return, she wanted to know that allowing a visitor was the right thing.

'I'll be all right,' Kate assured her, summoning an amount of courage from deep within. 'It is time that we started to emerge from our seclusion.' Rebecca nodded and went to do as she was asked.

The conversation between the Lasletts and their visitor was lacking in its normal level of light-hearted friendship, though Colin did not expect anything else. He was very aware of the sensitivity of the situation, and approached it accordingly.

'My mother wants to know if there is anything she can do for you,' Colin passed on the offer. 'She feels for you, having lost two children herself years ago.'

'It's a little hard, Colin,' Kate spoke unashamedly, her eyes glistening with unshed tears. 'Folk seem to feel that the baby is a subject better left unspoken about, but I want to talk about it. I know it is not the normal thing, but I'm desperate to talk with somebody about how I feel.'

'Would you like me to bring Mum over to the manse for a visit? I'm sure she would love to talk and pray with you.'

'Would you?' Kate hoped that this would be an answer to prayer.

'Any time you feel ready, I will bring her over.'

John didn't bother to intervene. He knew the social etiquette involved in a situation like this, but he also knew the very real grief that the parents of a stillborn infant bore, and their desperate need for comfort.'

The conversation lapsed for a few minutes, as they busied themselves with their cup of tea, and their own thoughts. Eventually Colin broke the silence.

'Have you heard how Miss Wallace is since her accident?'

John looked up from his cup, surprised at the turn in subject, and a little ashamed that he didn't know the answer.

'Accident?' Kate showed her ignorance on the matter.

'I'm sorry, dear,' John apologised. 'It happened the same day that Carlton was born. I have been so tied up with our own sorrow that I hadn't given Miss Wallace a second thought.'

'That's perfectly understandable.' Colin made the excuse for them.

'What happened?' Kate was almost thankful for the diversion this had given her thoughts. Colin spent some time telling the events that had occurred from the moment he had spotted the injured gelding, to the time he had finally left the Wallace estate. Even John hadn't heard the full account up until this point, and he began to see why his friend had become so enamoured of the young woman. But John was also disturbed to hear how Lady Wallace had treated Colin following the rescue. In fact, he was angry about it. Lady Wallace had taken a similar high-handed approach to Kate and her father on another occasion; an action that had caused a lot of resentment and grief.

'So Lady Wallace has not shown you any gratitude for your efforts?' John asked, unable to get past that point.

'I don't want to make any trouble, John. I only want to know that Miss Wallace is recovering properly.'

'Yes, well! There's more to this than you would be aware of, Col. Perhaps you could say it is a long-standing disagreement that has separated Lady Wallace and myself on more than one occasion.'

'Perhaps we should visit Miss Wallace,' Kate suggested, herself ashamed that the young girl had been overlooked during an intensely difficult period in their own family.

'Yes! I think it is high time that this matter was discussed.' John looked set for battle.

'Please! Don't make a fuss on my account,' Colin entreated. 'Just knowing that Miss Wallace is well will be thanks enough.'

'And you shall know exactly how she is progressing, Col, because I intend to take you with us. Lady Wallace needs to have the opportunity to offer her gratitude to you personally.'

John had sent word to Lady Wallace that they would be coming to visit, but he had not mentioned that they would be bringing her niece's hero with them. Colin had objected, of course, with an act he had thought was reasonably convincing. But even while his logic urged him to stay at home, he gave in to John's plan without too much resistance. Colin pushed the sensible thoughts to the back of his mind, in hopes that they would not convict him. He knew that he should not be feeding this fascination that he felt for Emily Wallace. He knew that nothing could ever come of it, no matter which way he looked at it; and yet, the desire to see her was so strong that John's suggestion was all the argument he needed to let go of a previously formed conviction.

As to the wisdom of wearing the borrowed suit yet again, he did not seem to have the mental energy to analyse it.

Much to Colin's amazement, he found himself all nerves as they pulled up outside the Wallace mansion. John had indicated some of what they might expect as a reception. He hadn't seemed overly confident that Lady Vera would be pleased to see him, and yet John was determined that the point should be made. And the point was that Mr Colin Shore had gone to a great deal of trouble on behalf of the young Lady Wallace, very possibly having saved her life, and John felt it was not just polite, but rather necessary that he be properly thanked.

As minister of the Green Valley Parish, John had overlooked Lady Wallace's insufferable pride on numerous occasions; and yet there had been times when he had done just as he planned to do now. If he felt that she had overstepped the bounds of common decency, actually being rude to one of the Valley's poor to their face, he had insisted, on more than one occasion, that she recognise her fault. Such exercises didn't often yield much fruit in the way of overt apology. Sometimes, Lady Vera might begrudgingly admit error.

'I don't think Lady Wallace was expecting three of you to tea,' Alice nervously chattered as she showed the party into the front hall. 'She only spoke of the Reverend and his wife.' Alice cast a sulky glance in Colin's direction, as if to inform him that his presence was unwelcome.

'Please let Lady Wallace know that we are here.' John chose to ignore the indirect reference to Colin.

It only took a few moments for the grand lady to make her entrance, which she did with all the regal style and grace of one of the royal family. 'Please come into the morning room, Reverend,' she invited, waving her hand in that general direction. 'I trust you will excuse me while I deal with this man.' It was plain that she was referring to Colin.

'Pardon us, Lady Wallace,' John spoke with diplomacy, 'but Mr Shore has accompanied us upon my invitation. I know you will welcome the opportunity to express your gratitude for the service he has given your niece.'

'I want no such opportunity,' Lady Vera snapped. 'If he is so determined for a reward, I'll have my man give him five pounds on his way out.'

'I don't want your money,' Colin burst out, furious at the prejudice directed his way. John placed a firm hand on Colin's arm as a sign to leave the talking to him.

'Mr Shore has every right to be offended by your attitude, Lady Wallace.'

'I'm offended that he has had anything to do with my niece, whatsoever.'

'She would have died if I hadn't found her.' Colin could not contain his fury. 'I found her injured and scared, and not all of her fright was from the accident, either.'

'That will do, Col!' John saw that he needed to take control of the situation. 'Lady Wallace knows very well how much she owes you. She is just being stubborn. Isn't that right?' John directed the question to the lady in question.

'Call it what you will, Reverend, but I would thank you to have this man removed from my house. He has his money. He can want nothing more with us.'

'I regret to say that we have all come together,' John went on confidently, well practised at this type of verbal sparring. 'Since you insist that Mr Shore cannot stay, we must all be on our way. Please convey our best wishes to your niece. I do hope she has recovered from her ordeal.'

John began to lead his wife and friend from the entrance hall, knowing that he had delivered his opinion and yet aware that there was nothing else to be gained by further argument. Colin was still agitated, but bowed to the wisdom of his counsellor. Kate was saddened. She had seen Lady Wallace direct a similar barrage of words at herself, and at a time when she was most vulnerable. It had been a hard time where Kate had fought to find forgiveness in her heart. That alone had taken quite some time; and it was even longer before Lady Wallace was eventually able to swallow her pride and accept that she had been wrong. Kate turned to follow her husband from the mansion, but had only gone two or three steps when they were all arrested by the sound of Emily coming down the staircase.

'Oh! I am so glad you have come!' Emily exclaimed. 'Don't tell me you have already had tea without me!' She cast an accusing eye at her aunt. 'You can't go until I've had a chance to talk with you for a while.'

'I'm sorry, child,' Lady Vera spoke sternly. 'Reverend Laslett has to go now. They are unable to stay for tea.'

'Oh!' Emily seemed genuinely disappointed. 'I understand, I think.'

Kate knew that Emily had assumed that they were still in a period of mourning. She could see the look of sympathy in the girl's eyes, and could not bear the falseness of the situation.

'I am feeling a lot better now,' Kate offered, even though the question remained unasked.

Emily allowed tears to spill down her cheeks. 'I was so upset when I heard,' she allowed her heart expression, ignoring her aunt's hard look of disapproval. 'I cried and cried for you. You must have been heartbroken.'

'That's enough, Emily,' Lady Vera cut into the open display of condolence. 'Now is not the time to be talking about such things.'

'How have you been?' Kate was committed to easing the atmosphere. 'Mr Shore told us how badly you were hurt.'

It was the first time that Emily had heard any reference to the silent man standing at the back of the group, but she had been aware of his presence from the first, and had only waited for this moment to lift her eyes to him.

'I don't know how to thank you, sir,' Emily continued to speak with full emotion. 'I don't know what would have happened to me if you hadn't found me.'

'Enough of that nonsense, child,' her aunt cut her off again. 'One of my servants would have found you eventually, and you would have been perfectly all right.'

'I'm sorry we have to leave,' John finally spoke up in apology. 'We are all very relieved to see you looking so well. I hope it won't be too long before you will be able to pay us a visit at the manse, again.'

'Oh, I'd love to . . . if you're sure.' Emily's loneliness was highlighted by this comment, and all of the visitors recognised it.

'There will be plenty of time later.' Lady Vera was determined to finalise the conversation and see the visitors on their way.

As the party of three set out from the Wallace estate, each nursed their own thoughts for a portion of the trip. John knew that he had hit the same stone wall he'd encountered on other occasions, but felt that he had made his convictions clear enough. He hoped that time would wear away the lady's stubborn prejudice.

Colin knew that he had no right to expect anything more of Lady Wallace. Her reputation had warned him of the futility of hoping for more. And it was futile. Thinking, dreaming, caring about Emily Wallace was a futile exercise. No matter how captivated he was by her innocent, pleading eyes, there was no future in dwelling on her in his mind, and he resolved there and then that he would not waste any more effort trying to see her again. It was better, he decided, to put distance between himself and anything pertaining to the Wallace Estate.

Kate felt a mixture of emotions. The trip out and visit, no matter how brief, had been a first step out of seclusion for her. It had been necessary and important, and she was glad that it was over. But mixed with the satisfaction on this score was an unsettled feeling. She didn't bother to get tangled up with the pointless anger she could have felt at Lady Wallace's action. She had done that before, and it had gotten her nowhere. This other feeling was something akin to alarm. Kate knew the signs of infatuation and Emily Wallace was infatuated with Colin Shore, if ever she had seen a case of it. What was worse, she suspected that Colin might possess his own version of admiration. If her marriage to John had been an unlikely and difficult prospect, this one was absolutely impossible. Kate didn't want to say anything in case she was imagining the whole thing, but she decided that she would keep a sharp eye out for further signs. *Such feelings can come to no good*, she thought to herself.

CHAPTER 8

J ohn was on his way home from a pastoral visit. He had taken food to a family whose mother had been taken seriously ill. Kate had helped Rebecca make up some bread and pies, and John had taken it out, with the intention to pray for her while he was there. The father was clearly grateful for the help, and for the encouragement the minister brought with him.

Now, as John rode back towards the manse, he decided that he would take an extra hour to look in on Colin and his family. The Shore farm lay on the direct route back home, so it seemed logical enough to pay the visit. John had not seen Colin in the two weeks since they'd made the trip to the Wallace Estate.

Mrs Shore was delighted to have the reverend call, and she instantly busied herself making a cup of tea. 'Go outside and see how far away Col is,' she ordered her youngest daughter. 'Tell him that Reverend Laslett is here to see us.'

During the time it took June to run across the house paddock and deliver the message, John chatted with the elder daughters and the mother. He heard about Julianne's developing plans for the future, though she lamented that she still had some time to wait before Pete felt ready to leave his father.

'I, for one, am glad he's not ready to leave yet,' Rose Shore spoke with conviction. 'The girl doesn't seem to realise that once she's married, the pair of them will probably never come back to Green Valley again. I'm not so sure that I'm ready to give her up yet.'

Finally, Colin came in from the paddock, stamping the dust from his feet before he came inside. 'I'm sorry I won't have time to stop for long,' Colin apologised. 'Just time for a cup of tea. There's a job I want to finish before it gets dark, and with the winter coming on daylight'll run out early.'

John didn't really mind. He decided to walk back with Colin to his job, as he wanted to ask him a few questions on his own.

'I hope you didn't take Lady Wallace's attitude too hard, Col,' John commented as they walked away from the house.

'I was angry at first, but then I remembered that she behaved just like her reputation.'

'There was just one thing that bothered me,' John was obviously tentative in broaching a delicate subject.

'Go on.'

'There was a comment you threw at Lady Wallace that I didn't quite understand. Something about Miss Wallace being afraid of more than the accident.'

Colin suddenly realised that he had let slip something that he should have kept to himself, and he was caught for a response.

'Is Miss Wallace in some danger?' John pressed.

'Not at the moment,' Colin answered, wanting to discuss the issue, but still not certain whether he should.

'But she has been in danger? Was she . . . I mean, she didn't see you as a threat?'

'No! Well, yes, actually, at first.'

'Do you think you had better talk about it?'

'I think I want to, but . . . . '

'Does the problem include you? Have you done something you shouldn't have?'

'John!' Colin was annoyed that his friend could so thoroughly mistake his intentions. 'Miss Wallace has been attacked by one of her father's friends, as I understand it. When I first found her, she was all mixed up and confused. The bump on the head, you know. When I tried to help her, she confused me with the blackguard who'd hurt her before.'

'Oh, dear Lord!' John was genuinely grieved to hear this information.

'I wouldn't want to pray for him,' Colin burst out in response. 'I feel as if I could ram his teeth down his throat.'

'Is that all you know about the incident?'

'I don't know the full details. I don't want to know. But I've had to repent of some murderous thoughts, I can tell you.'

'Yes, I understand.'

'Do you think that your wife could talk to her about it? I mean, Miss Emily . . . Miss Wallace, that is, puts on this happy little face, but I saw what she really feels underneath the façade. She is afraid, and hurting. Her aunt wants to send her back to England, and the fellow is still there.' Colin's desperation was evident in his tone. 'I couldn't bear to think of her being sent back there.'

John paused to think about what had been said for a few moments, while Colin watched for his response.

'You know, Col,' John finally spoke again, 'my wife has the idea that you have feelings for Miss Wallace.'

'I told you that I do,' Colin's tone showed frustration.

'But I thought you told me that you were going to leave it. That nothing could ever come of it.'

'I did tell you that, and I meant it too. Nothing could ever come of it. But that doesn't mean that I have suddenly lost the attraction I've felt for her. It doesn't matter how hard I try, the girl haunts my thoughts.'

'Give it some time,' John counselled. 'In the meantime, just keep your distance from her. I don't have to go into all of the difficulties that such a situation would present if you ever tried to make a go of it.'

'No! You don't have to go into it,' Colin confirmed wearily. 'I could recite all of the objections to you in alphabetical order if you wanted.'

'It's not that I don't think you're good enough for her, you understand.'

'I understand!' Colin was tired of the hopeless conversation.

***

Kate was genuinely pleased to have Emily visit with her again. It had taken another two weeks following their ill-timed visit to the mansion, for Emily to talk her aunt into allowing her to go out.

Just as on previous visits, Emily chatted and laughed merrily. No reference was made to the loss of the baby, or to the accident. Kate was content to let both matters take their place in history, and for them to move on in friendship.

'You know, I've been thinking.' Emily's tone indicated that she had, in fact, been scheming, and Kate braced herself waiting for the idea that was to come. 'You know how stuffy Aunt Vera can be when it comes to entertaining?' Kate had nothing to do but to nod her acknowledgment of the fact. 'Well, I have always wanted to meet other young ladies in the area. Oh, of course I love you and your friendship,' she hurried on in her easy manner. 'It's just that there are so many other young people to socialise with. Isn't that so?'

'Whom exactly did you have in mind?' Kate thought she could guess where this was leading.

Green Valley

'Take Mr Shore's sisters, for example.'

'Emily!' Kate tried to sound patient, and not cross like her aunt was wont to do. 'Does this have anything to do with Mr Shore – his being somebody special to you?'

'Of course Mr Shore is special to me. He was one of the first friends I met when I arrived in Australia. I have always said that I wanted to meet his sisters. Right from the very start. You ask your husband.'

'Yes, I know, dear.' Kate felt as if she was losing ground. 'But you know that your aunt does not approve of your mixing with the Valley farmers.'

'I do not understand her attitude,' Emily pouted. 'Mr Shore is a fine young man. What is it about him that Aunt Vera objects to so much?'

'You have not seen just how poor Mr Shore really is, or his family. They have no wealth at all.'

'They have land. Anybody with land has to be somebody.' Emily revealed her ignorance as she spoke.

'Australia is a land of opportunity, Emily. In England, nobody but the nobility and gentry were able to own property. Here in Australia, even the poorest tenant has the opportunity to try his hand at being a farmer. Colin's people had nothing to start with and all they have now is the land. I love the Shores very much, but they never come to church.'

'Why not?' Emily was indignant.

'Because they are ashamed of what they have to wear.'

'Fiddlesticks!' Emily retorted. 'Everybody has at least one gown that is decent enough to be seen wearing in public.'

'You really don't understand, do you?'

'Of course I do.' Emily was being stubborn.

'I know that you are quite in love with Mr Shore,' Kate decided that she would try to broach the subject of her suspicions.

'And why not?' The younger woman gave a proud shake of her head. 'As I said, he is a fine young gentleman, and any woman would be proud to have him as a husband.'

'Emily,' Kate sounded desperate, 'Mr Shore may act like a gentleman sometimes, but he is not one by birth. He is a nobody.'

'You sound like my aunt,' Emily accused.

'I know, and I'm ashamed to admit it. I have nothing against Colin Shore at all. I quite like him, in fact, but I know what your aunt would say if she knew what was going on in your head.'

'What could she do?' Emily scoffed.

'She would have you on the first ship back to England.'

Emily was silenced by this comment. Of all the things in the world she dreaded, going back to England was on the top of the list.

'I think your willingness to accept folks for who they are, despite their lack of wealth, is a welcome attitude, Emily, but . . . ' Kate paused for courage.

'But what?'

'I don't think it is wise for you to throw yourself at Mr Shore.'

'Do you mean flirt?' Emily showed that she had seen more of the wicked side of society than Kate had hoped. 'The talk amongst the young ladies in society is that you simply must flirt if you're ever going to catch the man you want.'

'Emily!' Kate sighed patiently. 'First of all, we are not in England now. Secondly, such a thing is disgraceful and not at all Christian. I don't know what your mother could be thinking, letting you mix with such people.'

'My mother passed away when I was only six. Father has had a chaperone, some old dowager whose only interest is seeing me married as soon as is convenient.'

'Did she allow you to talk like this?' Kate asked.

'No! Of course not. But other young ladies talk. I have heard what they speak about in the cloakroom.'

'Well, just remember that such a thing is not acceptable here. Reverend Laslett would be shocked to hear you talk this way.'

'But what am I to do? I love Mr Shore. How will he ever know that I would welcome his attentions?'

'You could not love Mr Shore or any other man, Emily,' Kate scolded. 'Love is a deep and serious business. I suggest that what you are feeling is an infatuation. If you follow my advice, and stay away from the Shores, you will soon forget about him.'

'I don't want to forget about him,' Emily complained. 'I want to see him as much as possible, and I want to meet his family.'

'That's impossible!' Kate was floundering for a way to challenge the young woman's wilfulness.

'It's not impossible,' Emily contradicted. 'I have made up my mind. If you won't help me, then I will find my own way.' She challenged the minister's wife with a rebellious look. 'I will do it,' she added. 'Even if you think I'm awful.'

'Emily, I care about you,' Kate patiently argued. 'Even though I think highly of Mr Shore, I know that he is not for you. There is someone far more suited to your tastes and station in life.'

'Like Lord Derickson?' Emily spat out her disdain. 'He is old enough to be my father, and has been married twice already. And you don't know what he is like. Mr Shore is decent and honourable and caring. Lord Derickson is none of those things, and if I used the words that would really describe him, then you really would be shocked.'

'Please, Emily,' Kate was losing the last bit of ground she had left.

'I was scared to death of coming all the way out here to Australia,' Emily went on, 'but I came. I had to come. If I'd stayed, then . . . . ' She paused, a shadow of horror crossing her face showed her thoughts. 'I won't ever go back. I have found the man I want to marry, and everything recommends him. Even you can't disagree with that.'

'But he has nothing.'

'He is a Christian man who lives by his convictions. Besides, even the poorest of gentlemen in London has some family inheritance that they can exist on. I would sooner that than live with a man like Derickson.'

'Emily, I think you are wrong to demand your own way like this. I am certain that Mr Shore will not think very highly of your unseemly behaviour.'

'I know it.' Emily nodded. 'That is why I want to get to know his family. At least that way I can still see him, and he me.'

'That is devious, Emily.' Kate sounded displeased.

'What other way is there?' Emily asked. 'What else am I to do?'

'Leave Mr Shore, and his family, alone.'

'I can't. I am lonely for one, and I am scared my aunt will send me away. Mr Shore is the one person who makes me feel safe.'

'Mr Shore is only a man. If you are pinning all your hopes of happiness on him and a marriage to him, even if you are willing to make the sacrifices, you will soon find that you have made a mistake.'

'In what way?'

'Even if you found the best husband in the world, Emily, the loneliness and emptiness you feel inside can not be filled by him. Only God can fill such a void.'

'God! What has God to do with us?'

'Do you believe there is a God, Emily?'

'Of course! Why else would I sit through dreary sermons every Sunday?'

Kate raised her eyebrows in disapproval, as she caught Emily's slip.

'I'm sorry. I didn't mean your husband's sermons, of course. He is very interesting to listen to.'

'There is more to a relationship with God than sitting through an occasional sermon,' Kate lectured. 'There is a spiritual need inside all of us. We were born like that, like every person since Adam and Eve. Jesus Christ sent his Holy Spirit so that we could have that need met inside. The trouble is, many people just like you think that marriage or money or power, as well as other earthly things, can fill the void. I can tell you from experience, Emily, they can't. You ask too much, even of a man as good as Mr Shore. Not even he can take the place of the Holy Spirit.'

'But you married. Surely you don't think I should join a convent?'

'That is not what I'm saying at all,' Kate allowed just a little frustration in her tone. 'I'm saying that you should look to the Lord to meet your loneliness and fear. Don't go chasing after a man. The right husband for you will come along eventually. Just be patient.'

'Patience has never been one of my better qualities,' Emily admitted. 'Thank you for your advice, but I know I want to meet with the Misses Shore, and I still plan to do that.'

'Perhaps I will have to talk to your aunt about your wilfulness,' Kate threatened.

'If you do, then she will probably send me back to England. Please don't, Kate. Give me a chance to make new friends. If it will make you feel any better, I will promise not to flirt with Mr Shore. I will hardly take any notice of him at all.'

Kate didn't feel any better with this assurance. She could see that Emily was used to getting her own way, and only wondered that her father had even tried to arrange a marriage for her. She wondered just how bad this Lord Derickson really was, and just how cruel and unfeeling her brother Charles was.

'All right, Emily,' she finally conceded. 'If you will just wait until I have talked to my husband about this, then I will see if there is a suitable way for you to meet Mrs Shore and her girls.'

By the time that John and Kate had shared their own individual encounters of the day, a lot of opinion had been aired, and a disagreement had ensued.

'But I agree with you, John,' Kate argued. 'I don't think she should go out there either, especially not having heard how Colin feels about her. The situation is positively destined to develop into something more than any of us can handle.'

'Then don't take her.' John spoke as if this was the simple solution to the whole dilemma.

'I am happy to comply,' Kate answered, 'but please understand just how determined she is to succeed in this thing. She will introduce herself to the Shore family with or without my help. I don't know if you agree, but I would feel happier knowing that I can at least monitor her behaviour, maybe even prevent the sort of opportunity that might – how can I say – foster romance.'

'Perhaps we should tell Lady Wallace.'

'I think she should know, John,' Kate agreed, 'except that it is likely that Emily will be sent back to England.'

'Not after what Colin told me today. Things are not safe for the girl at present.'

'Are you going to tell Lady Wallace about what has happened?'

'I doubt that Lady Wallace would acknowledge any truth in it. She is from the old school – such happenings are not talked about, and it is best to marry the girl off as soon as possible to avoid any disgrace that might arise out of such an incident. No, I don't think Lady Wallace would face that threat with any real sense.'

'Then please tell me, what do you think is the wisest course of action for me to take in regard to our young friends.'

'Lord forgive me if I'm wrong,' John offered as a half prayer, 'but I think you had better introduce Emily to the Shores, and I will recommend that Colin make himself scarce when you make the visit.'

'Other than this wild infatuation that the pair of them seem to have for one another, I don't see that there should be any objection to Emily making the Shore girls' acquaintance, do you?' Kate asked.

'I don't have any objections, but I can guarantee that Lady Wallace will be livid when she finds out.'

Emily arrived at the manse almost an hour earlier than previously arranged. She was full of excitement and had dressed in one of her prettiest day gowns. Her hair showed all the evidence of time and attention, and Kate sighed, knowing that all of Emily's hard work was about to be undone.

'But why?' Emily complained, when Kate strongly suggested that she change her dress and her hairstyle. 'This visit is important to me.'

'You may go as you are, if you wish, but Mrs Shore and the girls will be so thoroughly intimidated that it is unlikely they will ever invite you back again.'

'I don't understand!' Emily's confusion told on her face.

'I know you don't,' Kate sighed. 'I have tried to tell you that before, but you would insist.'

'Won't they be insulted if I dress in something like that?' Emily pointed with disdain at an old work dress that Kate had laid out on the bed for her to wear.

'They would more likely be insulted if you arrived wearing what you have on. I hope you will see what I have been trying to tell you all along,' Kate murmured. 'When I say the Shores have nothing; I mean nothing.'

Emily began to comprehend the seriousness of the family's plight, but she did not dare admit that she was wrong. With a slightly more sober attitude, she exchanged her own expensive satin and lace gown for the simple, brown, woollen dress.

Emily had asked Hodges to drive her for the day, and the older gentleman now accompanied the pair on their way out across the rolling foothills. He didn't make comment in Emily's hearing, but Kate knew that he was surprised at the way she was dressed, and more amazed when he learned where it was they meant to go.

'I hope Lady Wallace knows about this,' he muttered under his breath. 'There'll be a stir if she finds out after.'

Emily's excitement had dampened to some degree, but not her determination. *They think that I am not good enough*, she thought to herself. *I will show them that I can be every bit as good a farmer as I am a lady.* Just as Kate had said all along, Emily didn't really have any idea what it was that caused such a large gap between herself and Colin Shore. She had only ever mixed in aristocratic circles, and though she knew that other people existed, she had no notion just how. Even the servants who had attended her were always well dressed and polite. She knew that she was above them, but Mr Shore was nobody's servant. Mr Shore owned land.

But these preconceived ideas gradually began to erode the closer they came to the Shore property. Still, Emily's resolve remained firm, but her self-assurance – the pride with which she had maintained her justification – began to seriously waver. Kate began to point out features of the land that belonged to Colin, and began to talk of the family. It was when the house came into sight that Emily really began to be shocked. Kate saw her face pale, and her eyes widen with bewilderment, and while the minister's wife felt sorry for her at such a rude awakening, she was also glad. *Now she will let this silly infatuation go,* Kate thought. But Kate underestimated the power of stubbornness that Emily Wallace possessed. Emily had previously proclaimed that she was intent upon meeting the Shore family. She had made her intentions quite plain, and she was not going to be talked out of it. Even now, as she took in the tiny, ramshackle dwelling with the farm animals penned only yards away from the one entrance, Emily's pride bolstered her motivation to continue.

'We can turn around and go home, if you'd rather,' Kate offered gently, without malice.

'No, Kate! I said I wanted to meet Mr Shore's family, and I am determined to do it.'

'Very well.' Kate half-smiled at the obstinacy of the girl.

Rose Shore was delighted to see her minister's wife. They had developed quite a closeness during the period following the loss of Kate's baby. Rose had understood the younger woman's pain, and had known just what to do to help her through her time of sorrow. As she welcomed Kate inside, she offered a polite smile to the other young visitor – a smile which seemed to almost freeze on her lips when Kate introduced her.

'Mrs Shore, may I have the pleasure of introducing you to Miss Emily Wallace. She is visiting Green Valley from England.'

Rose was momentarily stunned. She had heard all about Emily Wallace. The local folk had whispered their versions of another proud lady to join Lady Wallace; her own daughters had talked about her status of being close to a princess; and of course, she had heard Colin's version of the accident and subsequent rescue. But never, in all of her imaginings did she think that young Lady Wallace would come to her doorstep.

'Mama!' Julianne's voice broke through Rose's mental fog. 'This is Miss Wallace, you know, Colin's Miss Wallace.'

'Yes! Yes, of course. I'm so sorry, Miss Wallace. Please forgive my rudeness. I never dreamed of seeing you here.'

Emily was a bundle of nerves herself. Here she was, dressed in servants' attire, standing in the smallest room she had ever seen, and roughly furnished at that, and yet she was drawn to Mrs Shore at once. The fact that the mother wore clothes that were in a worse state than the ones she wore; that her hair was roughly done, and already escaping the confines of the bun at the back of her head; the fact that there were four other girls, all similarly dressed, crammed into that one small kitchen, didn't seem to register as any worry in Emily's mind at all.

'I have so much wanted to meet you, Mrs Shore,' Emily found herself speaking in a small voice, 'and your daughters. I hope you don't mind the inconvenience of my dropping in unannounced like this.'

'The inconvenience!' Rose was astounded that she had been thought of at all. 'I am only sorry that I have nothing to offer you. We have not had a lot to spare for extra baking, you see.'

'We've brought some cake and scones from home,' Kate offered this information, 'that is if you don't mind us staying for a cup of tea.'

'Of course not. Please sit down.' Rose was flustered. Immediately she felt the shabbiness of her mismatched furniture. She could not think of a single chair in this kitchen/sitting room that would be good enough to offer a lady. Kate saw her dilemma, and sought to ease the tension.

'We will be quite comfortable at the kitchen table, Mrs Shore, if that is all right with you.'

'Yes! Yes of course. Please sit down.'

Julianne, of all the girls, seemed to be the only one who had the presence of mind to stoke the fire and fill the kettle. The three younger daughters were as hypnotised by the lady's presence as their mother was. Kate saw this, and was somewhat amused. Still, she tried her best to put the entire party at ease by chatting normally, and talking about the common things that involved them all.

The afternoon tea had moments of pleasure, but was constantly interrupted by clashes of culture that would inevitably bring everyone's eyes to Kate for a judgement on the issue. Emily had no idea that her finishing school etiquette was such an intimidating factor. She was so comfortable with the Shore family that she was quite unaware of her verbal blunders that actually seemed to them almost a criticism.

'I never new that people so poor could ever exist,' Emily commented thoughtlessly.

'Emily,' Kate spoke quietly, but the firmness in her tone could not be mistaken. 'This family and many others like them have lived happily for many years. Wealth is not everything in this world.'

'Oh, I know,' Emily reddened. 'Pardon me, Mrs Shore. I didn't mean any offence.'

'That's all right, dear.' It hadn't taken Rose long to see Emily as just another impulsive young woman, not unlike her own daughters. There were differences in speech and differences in table manners. There was even a marked difference in the way Emily conducted herself, having spent many hours in deportment lessons, but Rose liked her. Her thoughtless remarks could have been offensive if they had been accompanied by a sense of superiority and pride, but Emily Wallace's heart was pure, and Rose thought she could see why her son was so infatuated with her.

Colin had not ever told Rose his feelings, but she was his mother. She could tell what it was that had caused him to be so absent minded, and now, actually meeting the woman, she had to agree that she was indeed very beautiful. *It's a shame that nothing could ever come of it,* Rose thought. *I like this girl very much.*

CHAPTER 9

A s Emily drove away from the Shore farm she was full of happiness. She had liked Mrs Shore from the first moment, and Julianne and Christine in particular had seemed very willing to be open with her. The only disappointment about the whole day was that she had not seen anything of Colin Shore. Still, Emily had promised that she would not appear brazen, and for the moment, she was content to glory in the victory of having formed new friendships. She chatted gaily about the day's events with Kate as they travelled back to the manse.

Unfortunately, Kate had hoped that the visit would have actually quashed her enthusiasm, not encouraged it. Now, she knew that she must face her husband with the news that Emily had invited Mrs Shore and the two elder daughters to the manse for afternoon tea. Kate didn't know what to think. In her heart, she was pleased that Emily had not displayed a snobbish attitude, and that she was willing to embrace even those who were not from within her own class. But Kate did question Emily's motives. Somewhere, she knew, Emily entertained this fantastic idea of loving the son and brother, but the question Kate had to ask herself was whether Emily was really as devious as that. She appeared open and happy to meet the Shore women. She gave the impression that she enjoyed their company, and that she really looked forward to seeing them again. Could Emily really be putting all that on as a way of getting close to Colin? Kate was confused on the issue, and had nothing to do but wait to see if this façade would crumble or prove to be genuine affection.

In the meantime, Kate struggled with the issue of guilt. Somehow she felt certain that she really should have discussed the whole affair with Emily's aunt, yet she was somewhat afraid that Lady Vera would not think for a moment before packing off to her father, the girl who was now so dear to her. Such an action, by other accounts, could place Emily in worse danger. John allayed her attack of conscience for a while by telling her that he fully intended to talk to Lady Vera about Emily's wild notions, but he was looking for the right opportunity, and hoped that he could gain a sensible ally rather than an overreactive opponent.

'So long as she didn't see anything of Colin,' John said again. 'I've spoken to him in no uncertain terms about keeping away from her.'

'I confess,' Kate went on in conversation, 'I thought she would turn tail and run when she saw the house and farm, but to her credit she pushed on, and eventually managed reasonably well in her attempt at mixing with those beneath her.'

'Do you really believe the Shores are beneath the Wallaces, Kate?' John asked.

'According to the rules of society, yes. That is the way it is. What can we do to change it, John? I don't say that I hold to the idea, but I do admit that those rules are quite binding. Don't you remember your mother's attitude toward me?'

'I remember,' John gave a grim sort of smile. 'She was scandalised to find I'd married a nobody, and without money as well.'

'It would only be worse for Emily and Colin.'

'But you have to admit that they would make a lovely couple, don't you think, Kate?'

'No! I won't even consider the idea,' Kate slapped John's arm playfully. 'Just the thought could put me into a match-making mood that might bring disastrous consequences.'

'But you considered me, when you shouldn't have, didn't you?'

'Yes! And look at the disastrous consequences!' Kate laughed.

'All I can see is a beautiful wife, and two beautiful daughters whom I love very much. If that's disaster, then I'm all for it!' John declared.

Colin came in from his work only after the sun had completely disappeared from the sky. He was cold, and stamped his feet on the veranda as much to warm his frozen feet as to shake the mud from his boots.

'Guess who came to visit us today?' Thirteen-year-old June threw the question at her brother the moment he walked through the door.

'Don't know,' he answered without interest. 'What's for dinner?'

'It was that princess lady!' Six-year-old Harry was delighted to be the one to share the exciting news. 'She was very, very beautiful, and she talked like a princess, and walked like a princess.'

'Yeah! But she didn't dress like a princess,' June threw in, half in disgust. 'But she told us she would next time we met.'

'What are you two babbling about?' Colin asked, suddenly suspicious.

'Your lady, Miss Wallace, has been to visit.' Christine took delight in taunting her brother with the 'your lady' association.

'My lady!' Colin retorted. 'Christine!'

'Leave him alone, Christine,' Rose broke in. 'Miss Wallace graciously came to afternoon tea with us, Col.'

'Here?' Colin sounded horrified. 'Was she alone?'

'No! She was with Mrs Laslett,' Julianne joined in, 'and what do you mean, 'Here!' Don't tell me you're ashamed of us!'

'Will you girls leave your brother alone,' Rose admonished again.

'Where on earth did you put her? What did you give her to eat?'

'See!' Julianne captured her mother's attention. 'He is ashamed of us.'

'Well, anyway, Mr High-and-Mighty, we have been invited to tea at the manse with Miss Wallace. So there! She came to see us, not you.' Christine was feeling particularly spiteful.

'I didn't say she did come to see me,' Colin defended himself. 'And you're not going to tea at the manse.'

'Mum!' Christine wailed for support.

'Who do you think you are, telling us we can't accept an invitation? Just because she didn't invite you!' Julianne sounded furious.

'Will you children stop your bickering!' Rose's voice had reached a higher pitch in her attempt to gain authority. 'I have accepted on your behalf, girls, and Miss Wallace did invite your brother, if you must know, only I said he would most likely be too busy to come.'

'And they can't go either,' Colin added, as if the issue was closed.

'I'm sorry, son,' Rose spoke to Colin as if he were still a small boy. 'I have accepted, and we will be going.'

'How can you?' He seemed quite distressed about the prospect.

'What reason do you have that we shouldn't go?' Rose asked.

'Look at you. I can't afford new boots for me, and mine are nearly worn out. How on earth could I find the money to buy new dresses for you all?'

'Dress was not an issue, as I understood it,' Rose spoke calmly.

'Of course it's an issue,' Colin maintained. 'Miss Wallace would expect you to be dressed in an appropriate manner.'

'Like she was dressed today, perhaps?'

'Possibly. I have never seen her that she isn't always dressed up in fine silks and suits.'

'Well, she wasn't today,' Christine added for good measure. 'She had an old, brown work dress on. So there! She obviously doesn't care as much as you think she does.'

Colin was surprised to hear this piece of information, and perhaps a little confused. 'Are you sure it was really Miss Wallace who came to visit?' he asked, scepticism definitely in his tone.

'She was with Mrs Laslett. Why would the minister's wife lie to us?' Julianne was happy to have something to keep the argument going.

'It just doesn't sound like her, that's all.' Colin sounded distant and thoughtful.

'Perhaps you don't know her as well as you thought,' Christine added enjoying her temporary position of superiority. 'She has expressed great interest in becoming our special friend. I think she is very kind, and I intend to give her as much attention as she wants.'

'I don't think that's wise.' Colin was back from his thoughts and clear about what he felt. He knew all of the variables involved, not the least being John's advice for him to keep a wide berth of the young lady. Though his very soul yearned for closeness, he was determined to starve that feeling to death. John was quite right in his advice. Colin had never tried to contradict it. Even if Lady Wallace applauded the idea of someone as poor as himself courting her niece, he could not back it with any logic.

As much as his mixed up emotions cried against it, Colin refused on principle to offer a run down, overcrowded farmhouse to a woman who was used to marble halls and crystal chandeliers. Colin already hated himself for not providing better clothing and furniture for his own mother and sisters – women who were used to such conditions. How on earth could he possibly suggest that someone as fine as Emily Wallace exchange all of her luxurious existence for a large serving of poverty. He couldn't do it; he wouldn't do it; not while he was still in possession of some form of reason.

'What is it that bothers you so much about us sharing afternoon tea with Miss Wallace?' Rose's voice intruded into Colin's reflections. But his mother's question was not an easy one to answer honestly.

'I just don't think it's wise, that's all,' Colin repeated.

'But why?' Rose persisted. 'If Miss Wallace has no objection mixing with us, why should we object to her company?'

'Lady Wallace wouldn't like it!' Colin was glad he had thought of that excuse. He was getting close to the real reason, and he didn't want to voice that one out aloud.

'Do you think that Miss Wallace is extending these invitations without Lady Wallace's permission?' Rose took up this thought.

'I would be almost certain of it.'

'But Mrs Laslett wouldn't encourage such a thing, surely. Would she?'

'I don't . . . perhaps . . . I couldn't say.' Colin was stumped on this one.

'When we go over to the manse next week, I'll ask Mrs Laslett about it. I wouldn't want to be doing any underhand thing.'

There was nothing left for Colin to say without admitting the entire extent of his involvement in the situation, and so he had to let the matter drop, knowing that his sisters were going to build a relationship that would not be easily broken.

One afternoon tea had been followed by another, and then another; this time Emily came back to the Shore farm. Rose had asked about Lady Wallace's permission, and had found out that Emily was acting on her own. Rose had made some strong objections, supported by Kate, and Emily had finally agreed that she would not socialise with them any more until she had gained her aunt's wholehearted permission. Kate had believed that this would be the end of the whole relationship, and was very much surprised that Emily had returned full of plans for the next engagement. Kate didn't want to accuse Emily of lying, as such, and so she told her that she was going to send her husband to make sure that Lady Wallace understood all that was going on. John paid the visit to the isolated figurehead, and returned with some very interesting news. Just as Kate had imagined, Lady Vera was most definitely opposed to her niece's ideas of mixing with the lower-class farming families, but had confessed to a weakness where Emily was concerned.

'Your niece is manipulating you,' John spoke plainly.

'I know it,' Lady Vera confessed. 'You don't know, Reverend, just how lonely I have been all these years since my husband has passed on. Having the child with me has been like a new lease of life, though I would never admit that to her face.'

'But you let her have her own way all the time.'

'What is there that I can do to stop her?' Lady Wallace asked.

'We both thought you would threaten to send her back to her father,' John answered.

'I've threatened, but the child knows I have no intention of doing anything of the kind. I would miss her too much.'

John was both amused and concerned at the way the older woman allowed her niece to have her own way, even though he didn't always agree with Lady Vera's prejudiced opinions.

And so John and Kate watched with concerned interest at the way Emily's relationship developed with Julianne and Christine, in particular.

One day, several weeks later, John found himself again talking to Colin about Emily.

'I can't help seeing her,' Colin bemoaned the fact. 'Every time I turn around she seems to be taking a walk with one of my sisters, or bringing something to my mother. And the girls never stop talking about her. How on earth am I supposed to put her out of my head?' He sounded very frustrated.

'The thing is, Colin, Miss Wallace thinks she is in love with you.' John felt it was time to lay all of the cards on the table.

'What! That's impossible!' Colin shook his head as if in denial. 'How could she think that, especially when she's seen the way we live and all that?'

'Apparently, she isn't particularly concerned with the way you live.'

'That's ridiculous!' Colin wanted to brush the idea aside. 'You're not suggesting that she is going to all this trouble with my family just so that she can get close to me?'

'I'm not suggesting it, I'm merely relaying what it is she has told my wife.'

Colin was speechless. If it weren't for his principles, he probably would have been terribly flattered, but as it was, John's words only served to anger him.

'I can't do anything about that,' Colin almost shouted, a few moments later. 'You know I can't. I haven't got anything to offer her. It would be stupid even to suggest it.'

John didn't say anything, only nodded his agreement.

'Can't you see how hard this is for me? I need to forget her, and yet I can't, not with her constantly throwing herself at me.'

'I don't think that is quite fair,' John spoke calmly. 'Miss Wallace has been very careful to observe protocol. She only wants you to know that she is alive. That's all.'

'That's all! Alive! She affects the very air I breathe. Either she has to go, or I'm going to go mad.'

'Perhaps you need to tell her that.'

'Me?' Colin exploded in frustration. 'I'm not going to speak one word to her, because I'm afraid of what I will say.'

'Then do you want Kate to talk to her. Perhaps she can explain the situation to her.'

'Do you think she could? I don't want to hurt her feelings, John, but this has got to stop.'

John left the exchange feeling frustrated himself. He understood Colin's situation and limitations, and he also understood just how much he felt for the young lady. But despite all of this, nothing had changed. There was still no way that the two young people could ever find a suitable way to fulfil their feelings. Emily was going to have to understand and co-operate.

But Emily wasn't willing to understand.

'But why doesn't he like me?' Emily cried, when Kate had spoken about the situation to her. 'I have tried to behave and act just like his sisters.'

'It's not that,' Kate tried to explain. 'There is just too much distance between you, Emily.'

'I thought perhaps he liked me a little bit,' Emily sounded hurt. 'He has always been so very kind to me before.'

'Oh, he likes you very much,' Kate reassured. 'But nothing can ever come of the relationship. That's why you have got to stop seeing his family. It confuses everything.'

'How?'

'Mr Shore likes you, but he needs to forget about you, and when he keeps seeing you all the time, he feels that it's impossible.'

'But I don't want him to forget about me. I want him to think about me all the time. I think about him all the time.'

'Emily, that is fairytale romance. It isn't practical, and it isn't going to happen in this instance. You need to be mature about this. You will be eighteen soon, and you can't act like a spoiled child for the rest of your life.'

'But I'm not trying to. I don't mind giving up all of the servants and clothes. I would do anything for him.'

Kate sighed. She felt as if she were talking in circles and getting nowhere.

Colin could see that Kate Laslett had not made any impression if she had talked to Emily. Julianne and Christine continued to see the young lady, despite Colin's own objections.

'You are acting like a real grump,' Christine accused him on one occasion. 'Anybody would think that you were actually jealous and wanted to see her for yourself.'

That comment had hit a little too close to home, and from that day on, Colin had decided to take a different approach.

He knew he wasn't being honest, or entirely fair, but he was determined to stop the craziness that was driving him to the edge of sanity. One Sunday afternoon, after he'd led his family in prayer and Bible reading, Colin set out for a ride, several miles, to the Miller farm. This time, it was not Ned Miller that he was going to see, but rather Ned's father, Walter.

'Haven't seen you in a number of months,' Walter commented dryly. 'Hope your crops are doing well.'

'We've had a good rain,' Colin added to the small talk. 'So long as the frost doesn't do any damage, and we don't see any locusts, I'm hoping for a reasonable harvest.'

'What about hay? You got plenty of feed for your animals?'

'The season looks good so far. The animals are holding a fair amount of condition.'

Colin was getting impatient with the talk about the farm and wanted to come straight to the reason for his visit.

'Well, what is it, boy?' Walter Miller prompted, once he realised Colin had something to say.

'I . . . ah . . . I was thinking . . . that is, I wanted to know if . . . .'

'You want to come courtin' my daughter, Kathleen,' Walter guessed. 'There's been talk of it. That's to say, Ned thought you might be interested.'

Colin was relieved that Walter had said the words for him. This was his intention, but his motives were so false he didn't have the heart to actually speak the words.

'I haven't got any objections,' Walter went on. 'You work hard enough, and I'm sure that the pair of you could breed up some good strong children.'

Colin hated the thought, but he nodded his head anyway.

'Why don't I get the girl to come on outside, and the two of you can talk about it.'

Walter got up from his seat on the veranda, and went inside to get Kathleen. Colin felt ashamed of himself, proposing marriage to a girl he didn't love and didn't really want, but it was the only way, he felt, that he could shake Emily from his thoughts, and he hoped from his life.

Kathleen Miller was a tall, spindly girl, and just as strong as any farmer could want for a daughter or a wife. When she came to stand on the veranda, Colin was stuck for a way to begin a conversation, but Kathleen was happy to take the initiative. 'Dad says you wanted to ask me something.'

Colin tried not to compare her plain, rugged speech with the bell-like, rounded tones he was so in love with.

'I've been thinking, maybe you wouldn't mind if I came courting.' Colin felt like the fraud he was, but went on anyway.

'Of course I wouldn't mind. Been waitin' for you for a long time.' Kathleen's smile was genuine and full of pleasure, which only added to Colin's shame.

He sat and listened to Kathleen's happy talk of farm life, and hopes for a large and happy family, and how much she had longed to get married, with him hardly adding a word. When he left the Miller farm, he felt miserable, and yet satisfied that he had taken the positive action he needed to. The only trouble was, his satisfaction came at Kathleen's expense. Colin wondered if he would ever come to love her or desire her as much as he had desired Emily Wallace.

CHAPTER 10

*I*t hadn't taken more than a few days for the word to get out. Kathleen Miller was thrilled beyond words, hardly even noticing that her suitor seemed less than enthusiastic. Kathleen's sister-in-law, Lilly, had promoted Colin Shore to such an extent previously, that Kathleen was quite ready to accept that she had landed the best catch in the district. Her excitement easily made up for the lack of passion that would have been obvious to anyone else. By the time Colin had paid his second visit to the Miller farm, Kathleen had already told Lilly of the joyous news. Though Colin had not actually proposed yet, Kathleen had jumped several steps ahead and had already begun to plan as if this was a forgone conclusion. Lilly was as pleased as she could be, considering her heavy pregnancy. She had hoped that something would eventually work out between her sister-in-law and her husband's closest friend. She eagerly shared the news with Ned, who was equally happy, and who wasted no time in offering his congratulations.

'So! Finally, we are to be brothers!' He clapped Colin on the back in a good-natured gesture of affection. 'You've taken your time making up your mind.'

Colin found it very hard to respond to all of the enthusiasm. His dishonesty of heart was plaguing his conscience, and yet he was determined to see the course he had chosen through to its horrible end. He still hoped that perhaps he might miraculously fall in love with

Kathleen Miller, though the more he saw of her, the more he doubted it.

Still, the ripple effect of good news didn't end there. Because Lilly had been unwell in the last few months of carrying her third baby, several young women of the district had taken it in turns coming to keep house and mind her two children for her. Kathleen, of course, had already been several times this week, and her visits had been followed by Julianne Shore, who'd also offered to help out. Unable to so much as get up from her bed, Lilly Miller had nothing to do but talk, and she wasted no time in bringing up the subject of the newly formed couple.

'Where on earth is your mother going to put Kathleen when they marry?' she asked Julianne, who stood wiping crumbs off the breakfast table.

'Kathleen?' Julianne was surprised. 'When she marries who?'

'Colin, of course!'

'Colin!' The surprise only increased.

'Don't tell me he hasn't even told his own family. That would be just like him.'

'Told us what?'

'Colin has proposed to Kathleen. She is absolutely wild with delight. You should see her!'

Julianne opened and closed her mouth several times, unable to formulate a sensible response.

'Are you sure?' she eventually asked.

'You don't seem very happy about it,' Lilly observed. 'Don't you like Kathleen?'

'Oh, no! I mean, yes! I like Kathleen very well, it's just that . . . . '

'That what?' Lilly seemed concerned.

'Nothing.' Julianne thought better of voicing her thoughts. 'Don't worry about it,' she brushed the subject aside. 'I'm sure Colin will tell us all about it when he's ready.'

But Colin didn't have a chance to tell anybody else. The news spread like wildfire, and grew in grandeur as it passed from one to the other. By the time Emily heard about it, Colin was supposedly set to be married by the end of the month. Needless to say, she was devastated.

'I don't understand,' she wailed. 'I tried so hard to please him.'

Kate Laslett, who was the unfortunate bearer of the bad news, placed a comforting arm around the young lady's shoulders. 'There was just too much distance between you, Emily,' she tried to reassure. 'Mr Shore needs a wife who can cook and clean, and run the farm if necessary. There was never any way that you would have been able to do those things.'

'I will learn! If that's what it takes, then I will learn.'

'But it's too late now,' Kate objected. 'Mr Shore has decided to choose someone else.'

'I have to try.' Emily had discarded reason, and embarked upon an emotional display of determination. 'If he knows that I can be anything he wants in a wife, then perhaps he will reconsider.'

'Emily! That is not what you have been brought up to. Your father never intended that you should become a servant in your own home. Let's just forget about Mr Shore. Let him choose from among his own people, and you will eventually find someone from among your own people.'

'No!' She cried stubbornly. 'I won't give him up.'

'But he was never yours to give up, Emily. He never promised you anything, and you shouldn't be hoping like this. It's quite wrong!'

Kate instinctively knew that she had not convinced Emily of anything. She felt sorry that her young heart had been so broken, especially considering that she knew what Colin really felt about her. Not only that, but Kate was a little angry at Colin that he should be misleading his fiancée, allowing her to believe that he cared enough to marry her. Kate knew what he was doing, and though she also hoped that Emily would simply give up, she couldn't condone the way that he was treating Kathleen Miller. The whole situation was awkward and getting more difficult as each day passed. As Kate watched Emily ride away, she wondered just what foolish thing she would do as a reaction to the news she'd just heard.

A moment to be recorded in history occurred on that cold day, late in winter. Lady Wallace had never before condescended to visit anyone outside of her own circle of influence, and probably would not have chosen to do so now, had not the circumstances become so desperate. If Rose Shore had felt intimidated the first day that Emily Wallace had paid a visit, dressed in plain work clothes, she now felt totally reduced to a state of shock. Lady Wallace swept over her doorstep as if it were her own parlour to command. She had taken no trouble to dress in a less awe-inspiring manner so as to put the peasants at ease. She was not here to make anyone feel comfortable. She had come with the express purpose to set a few matters straight, and that was exactly what she intended to do.

'Now see here,' she dispensed with any polite greeting, and forged straight ahead. 'I want you to stop this nonsense with my niece right away.'

Rose was thoroughly overwhelmed by the awesome woman's presence, and had no words to agree or argue.

'She informs me that you intend to teach her how to be a farmer's wife. Is this true?'

'Not quite!' Rose's voice squeaked with fear.

'Bother it, woman. What have you promised her?'

'I find it very hard to deny her anything,' Rose admitted quietly. 'She has begged me to teach her, but I have not wanted to go against your wishes.'

'And what is this nonsense about her wanting to marry your son. What insolence! I always took him to be a conniving character.'

'Pardon me, Lady Wallace,' Rose's voice rose in defence. 'Miss Emily is, as she says, desperately in love with my son, Colin. But my son has never put one foot out of line. In fact, he is currently courting another young woman.'

'What! Isn't my niece good enough for the likes of him?'

'He knows that you would never have approved of such a marriage. He has always said that, and has never given Miss Emily any reason to hope otherwise.'

'Then what is all this nonsense. If he's engaged elsewhere, what does she think can be gained by learning how to cook?' She spat the word out as if it was distasteful.

'I am sorry.' Rose apologised. 'I don't mean to speak badly of Miss Emily, but she is rather headstrong. She is of the opinion that if she can just learn to do all the things I do, that Colin will change his mind about her.'

'And will he? Change his mind, I mean?'

'I don't know, your ladyship. My son is also quite headstrong, and very proud. But I think that he has taken the reverend's advice.'

'Which was?'

'Which was to let your niece alone, and not to encourage her.'

'Glad to hear somebody has kept a level head around here!'

'I like Miss Emily very much,' Rose offered. 'If it weren't for the huge difference in lifestyles, I would have been proud to have her as a daughter-in-law.'

'As if I would have allowed such a thing,' Lady Wallace sniffed with disdain. 'What do you intend to do about this foolishness of hers?' She barked the question at the terrified farmer's wife.

'What would you have me do?' Rose replied.

'You are the one who seems to have the most influence now. I think it must be up to you.'

'Me?' Rose sounded surprised. 'What influence do I have?'

'The child never stops talking about you,' Lady Vera sounded insulted as she spoke the words. 'If I hadn't seen you for myself, I might have believed that you were perhaps a supernatural apparition.'

Rose was truly amazed to hear the way Lady Wallace was asking for her advice and help. She had to listen carefully to the words spoken, because the tone of delivery had not changed. If Rose had interpreted by attitude alone, she would have felt thoroughly told off and abused, but Lady Wallace's actual words held a different message. By the time she'd finished, Rose believed that she had heard a plea for help.

'If I might be so bold as to suggest, and with your permission of course . . . ' Rose began tentatively.

'Well! What is it?' Lady Vera lost none of her impatient tone.

'I have a young neighbour who has been confined to bed these last weeks, and is likely to be there some weeks more until her baby is born. My daughters Christine and Julianne have been taking their turn at keeping house for her, and minding the other two children. I know it sounds awful to you, but perhaps your niece could take on that responsibility for a few days.'

'What are you suggesting? That she becomes a house servant?'

'It would only take one or two days, I'm sure. The work is hard and dirty. Miss Emily thinks that it is romantic, but once she is left all alone to complete the jobs without help, I'm sure she will begin to see just how unromantic being a farmer's wife really is.'

For a split second, Vera Wallace, herself, wondered just what it would be like to be responsible for her own food and clothes. It was not an idea that had ever crossed her mind before, as she had grown up with many servants, and had taken their services very much for granted. But she quickly shook off the disturbing thought and considered what the lowly housewife had suggested.

'Very well,' she finally assented. 'But I want this nonsense over and done with. I hope it won't take more than a week.'

'I hope so too,' Rose agreed, 'but I do have to confess, I will miss her when she returns to her proper life. She is quite a delightful girl in many ways.'

'And that is why she is still here, and not packed off to her father. I have to confess that I need the girl here. I cannot imagine how I ever lived without her.'

Rose smiled at the candid confession. She had looked beneath the sarcastic and harsh façade that the grand lady had so tried to portray, and had seen a lonely old woman, who in her own way was as likeable as her niece.

'Will you tell your niece about the plan?' Rose asked, just before Lady Wallace took her leave.

'It's likely you'll see her before I do, if she is up to current form.'

The funny thing was that neither Rose nor Lady Vera really believed that Emily would be put off from her quest by a little challenge like domestic work. Vera knew her niece's stubbornness too well, though she had hoped it might work. Rose had begun to recognise this tenacity. Emily had declared that she was motivated by love, but both women felt they knew better. Emily was in love with an idea. Something had happened on that night of the accident to cause the young lady to feel enamoured by Colin's presence. Rose hoped upon hope that nothing improper had occurred, but Colin had assured her that everything was perfectly in accordance with what was necessary. Still, Emily was smitten, and that, mixed with her determination, made Rose begin to doubt whether her plan would succeed.

Emily, naturally enough, was delighted to have one last opportunity to prove her worth. No obstacle seemed able to match her resolve to do that much. Julianne had accompanied Emily on her first day to the Millers'. Naturally, Emily had never lifted a hand to household chores before, but she paid close attention to everything that Julianne told her, and resisted every time she felt like wrinkling her nose in disgust. Changing the toddler's nappy was perhaps the most distasteful job of the morning, but by the end of the day, other tasks had presented themselves that proved to be just as awful.

'Have you had enough?' Julianne asked at the end of the first day.

'I said I would learn, and I will!' Emily stuck out her chin defiantly.

'Shall I send Christine along tomorrow, or do you think you can manage on your own?'

'Oh, please! I think I will need Christine, or someone, for another couple of days yet. I don't think I could get everything right on my own.'

Julianne smiled, and waved to her as she set out on her way home. Julianne had arranged for her brother to pick her up, and she climbed up onto the wagon seat.

'What has Miss Wallace been doing here?' Colin asked, suddenly suspicious.

'She's been helping Lilly.' Julianne was being deliberately vague.

'Helping Lilly! Why?'

'Because Lilly needs some help at the moment!'

'That's not what I mean,' Colin spoke angrily. 'I mean, why her?'

'Why not her?' Julianne was playing a difficult game, and she knew it.

'Ah! Forget it!' Colin slapped the reigns on the horses back. 'Don't tell me, Miss Wallace is going to walk all the way home.'

'I believe she said she was,' Julianne answered. 'It's not too far from here.'

'Not for you, maybe, but she's different!'

'Why is she different?'

'Julianne. You are being hard to get on with. I think you should ask Miss Wallace if she would like a ride home.'

'Why don't you ask her?'

'Because that wouldn't be proper, would it?'

The brother and sister bantered on like this for several more minutes before they overtook the walking figure.

'My brother wants to know if you'd like a lift home, Emily.' Julianne deliberately used the familiar name.

'No, thank you, Mr Shore.' Emily smiled sweetly. 'I haven't very far to go, and the exercise will do me good.'

Colin had no choice but to accept the excuse. He could not have known just how much those words had cost the young lady. She was bone-tired and aching from all the unfamiliar work of the day, and she longed to accept the ride; but she had nothing if she didn't have her pride, and she was determined to prove to him that she was every bit as tough as Kathleen Miller or any other farm girl.

The following days may not have yielded exactly what Vera Wallace had wanted where Emily was concerned. On the one hand, Vera mumbled her discontent. 'It's pure foolishness, child,' she ranted at Emily. 'Thank goodness your father doesn't know what you're up to. What a disgrace!'

But Emily paid her no heed. She was set on her course, and resolved to see her 'duty' through.

Secretly, Vera was proud of Emily. If her memory served her correctly, other young ladies of the *beau monde* would probably have fainted at the thought of lifting a hand to help themselves. If there had been one of them that would have voluntarily chosen to learn this particular craft, Vera knew that she probably would have come home complaining and crying before half the day had finished. Vera would not have let this admission be dragged from her, but she was proud of the way Emily proved herself to be made of tougher stock.

Of course, Vera didn't know that Emily was complaining and crying inside. The work was backbreaking for a novice, and Emily had never seen so much soil and filth at one time before. She had never dreamed what it was that the servants actually did to get rid of the household waste, and now that she knew, she had a whole new respect for them. Feeding food scraps to the pigs, emptying chamber pots, and tossing the ashes from the fireplace down the long-drop were all exercises that taxed Emily's willpower to the maximum.

But there were actually some chores that Emily found enjoyable. She enjoyed most of the jobs associated with the children, so long as they weren't messy, and she quite liked preparing the meals. Once Julianne and Christine had decided to leave Emily on her own, Lilly became quite the close companion and directed Emily on all of the ins and outs pertaining to cooking. It was creative and Emily found herself satisfied when loaves and stews turned out the way that they were supposed to. She would have been just as happy to leave the cleaning up to the servants, however, and she had to continually remind herself that she was the only servant in the house, and was therefore responsible for her own mess.

The two or three days turned into two or three weeks. Lady Vera had stopped pestering Emily about when she would stop her shenanigans and come home. Colin had stopped visiting with his friends, Lilly and Ned, and Emily had started to become used to the routine expected. She was pleased with herself, and while it was still a game, and not a lifelong vocation, she was happy to remain. She got on exceptionally well with Lilly, and began to look forward to the arrival of the new baby almost as much as Lilly did.

During their conversations together, Emily had heard about Lilly's sister-in-law, Kathleen. She knew that this was the woman who had captured Colin Shore's attention when she couldn't, and she wanted to hate her very much. But Lilly spoke so fondly of her, and sounded so happy that the pair were to be married that Emily made no comment at all about her own feelings on the matter. She tried to smile and sound interested when Lilly spoke of 'Kathleen and Colin'. She tried hard to quash the jealousy that she felt, but it was not until the other young woman actually made an appearance that Emily was finally able to deal with her wild emotions.

Kathleen had agreed to allow Emily to look after Lilly, and therefore had not been to see her sister-in-law for several weeks. But naturally enough, she and her parents wanted to know just how their son's family was getting along. So Kathleen arrived on the doorstep one morning, early in the spring, a basket of baked goods on her arm.

'You must be Emily,' Kathleen was open and genuine. 'I have heard so much about you. I know Lilly feels that you are indispensable.'

Emily didn't quite know how to take this comment. It was the first time that she had been congratulated as a servant, and given assurance that her position was secure. She wasn't quite sure whether she was happy about this.

'My name is Kathleen,' the visitor broke into Emily's thoughts. 'I'm Ned's sister. I hope you don't mind. Is Lilly up to seeing anyone?'

'I . . . yes . . . I'm sure she'd be happy to see you.' Emily was stunned at the sudden development, and was not sure of anything, least of all the way she felt. Kathleen brushed past her into the house, and Emily could see that she was far taller than any girl she had ever seen before. She did not have an ounce of fat on her, but her bones, hands and feet were like that of a small man, like someone of her brother, Charles', stature. Emily didn't know if she should feel superior or intimidated by this physical difference. She finally decided to let it go, and concentrate on other attributes that she was now able to observe firsthand. Though Emily would never have described Kathleen Miller as a beauty, there was something about her rival that was captivating. In the end, Emily decided that she was the most pure and unaffected girl she had ever met. Kathleen didn't try to put on any airs or pretensions for anyone. The person Emily saw conversing with her sister-in-law was exactly the person Kathleen was. She was happy, confident and generous in spirit. Emily detected that there was no meanness in her, and she suspected that Kathleen would never be so selfish as to demand her own way, as Emily knew she was constantly trying to do. By the time Kathleen had left, Emily felt totally ashamed of herself and of her attitude. She could easily see why Colin Shore had chosen Kathleen instead of her; and for the first time in months, she began to see sense. Why on earth was she insisting that he must notice her, Emily Wallace? Why hadn't she been able to see that there were other girls, girls like Kathleen Miller, who were not only more capable in domestic duties, but were more attractive in spirit? Emily wanted to go home there and then; she wanted to throw herself on her bed and cry her heart out. Her aunt had been right all along. She had been acting foolishly. She didn't belong in a farmhouse at all, and now she realised that she had been using people like Julianne and Christine merely to get her own way. Emily felt utterly wretched, having faced the full force of her own selfishness.

Lilly noticed the change in her demeanour, and guessed what it was all about. She had heard from Julianne all about Emily's infatuation, and while she had wanted to discourage her from it, she now felt the disappointment of the poor little rich girl.

'Would you like to leave everything and go home for the day?' Lilly offered kindly. 'I'm sure that Ned will manage when he gets home.'

Tears welled up in Emily's eyes, and she turned her gaze sorrowfully toward her companion. 'I want to,' she admitted softly, 'but I can't. I promised you I would help out until the baby comes, and I need to be a woman of my word.'

'That is a fine sentiment, Emily,' Lilly encouraged, 'except that I think you have finally seen some truth this afternoon, haven't you.'

Emily nodded.

'I wouldn't blame you if you decided that you didn't want to stay.'

Oh, Lilly!' Emily decided to throw caution to the wind and confide in this gentle soul. 'I have been such a selfish fool. I wanted so much to capture Mr Shore's attention that I didn't think of him, or of anyone else. I was only thinking of myself. But Kathleen is a wonderful girl, and I am nothing. Whatever will he think of me? Will any of you ever forgive me?'

'You've learned a powerful lesson, Emily,' Lilly spoke quietly, 'but you mustn't think that you're the only one who has ever been selfish. We have all had our turn at acting badly.'

'I don't think Mr Shore would ever act as badly as I have. He is too good a man.'

'I think you're seeing him through rose-coloured glasses, and though his mother's name is Rose, I think you know what I mean.'

'Oh, but I have seen how Mr Shore is. He is so considerate and kind, and honourable.'

'I know that he has these qualities Emily, but I assure you, he has his faults as well.'

'I would find that very hard to believe. I think your sister-in-law is a very lucky woman.'

CHAPTER 11

*I*f Emily could have known just how badly Colin could act, she would have been shocked; she truly believed that he was without fault. But the situation between him and Kathleen was coming to the point where his faults were about to become quite evident.

He had continued to ride over to the Miller farm, usually on a Sunday afternoon, but occasionally during the week as well. It was all a pretence on his part. He had no desire to see Kathleen at all, but he felt it his duty to make the effort, now that he had made this step towards engagement. Every other time that he had been, Kathleen had been thrilled to see him, and had entertained him with her chatter, and her good food. The conversations had been painfully one-sided, but Kathleen had been blind to this in her excitement.

But this fine Sunday afternoon was tending to take a different direction. Walter Miller suggested that the pair of them take a walk together, and he jokingly suggested that Kathleen might like to let Colin get a word in edgeways. Colin had complied with the suggestion, though he would have preferred to sit quietly in the Miller's kitchen and listen to their family talk. Still, the two young people set out away from the small home. Colin felt obliged to offer Kathleen his arm, which he did, and she accepted, but inside he was cringing at her touch. Silently, he berated himself. *Kathleen is a good and loving woman*, he recited to himself. *I have no reason on earth to be so unkind to her*. And yet he was unkind to her in his thoughts. He resented her intrusion into his life, and wished that he had never shown his face at the Miller place. Kathleen sensed his emotional distance and, for the first time in their relationship, she was determined to find out just what was going on in his head.

'Tell me what you're thinking?' she asked gently. 'I'm always chattering away about how I feel. What is it that you feel?'

Colin was caught. He didn't have a reasonable answer for her, and he couldn't tell her the truth. She saw his hesitation, and suddenly began to wonder.

'Colin, are you sure that you love me?'

'I have asked your father's permission to marry you,' Colin defended.

'That's not what I asked.' Kathleen said. 'Do you love me?'

'Love has many different expressions,' Colin hedged. 'I believe that commitment and faithfulness is the strongest part of love.'

'You're not answering me,' Kathleen's voice rose with the fear that had suddenly gripped her stomach. 'Do you feel anything for me, Colin? I have to know.'

Colin knew he was trapped. He felt nothing for her at all. The slight admiration he had once had for her character had eroded away because of the resentment he had allowed to grow – a resentment that was all of his own doing.

'You don't love me do you?' Kathleen was less accusing than she could have been. 'Why, Colin? Why did you come here in the first place? Surely you're not that desperate for a wife.' Still no answer came, and Kathleen became angry. 'I don't understand you at all. If you don't want to marry me, then say so. I could take that better than all of this . . . this . . . lying!'

'I didn't mean to lie to you,' Colin found some compassion. 'I shouldn't have come, but I was desperate. I did mean to marry you. I really did. And I still will.'

'No! You won't! I won't have you.' Kathleen's face showed her hurt and anger. 'I wouldn't have you if you were the last man on this earth,' she shouted.

'Kathleen,' Colin tried to placate her.

'What?' she snapped at him. 'What are you going to tell me? That you're sorry you made a fool of me? I don't ever want to see you again.' With these words said, Kathleen pulled away from him and hurried back toward her home.

Colin stared sadly into the distance. He had really made a mess of the whole situation. However could he explain what he had done? He now saw it plainly and simply. He didn't have the courage to tell Emily straight that he did not want to marry her, probably because he really did want to. It was more a case of that he *could not* marry her. Still, he had not told her. Instead, he had gone behind her back to another innocent girl, had promised her something he didn't have to give, and then crushed her in the process. Colin felt like a heel, and assumed that if he had asked for an opinion of any one of his friends, that they would probably have agreed. He was a heel.

It took longer for the news of the break-up to get around the Valley. Colin said nothing to his family. He was too ashamed of himself. Nor did Kathleen say anything to her family. She was distraught at first, and her mother assumed that there had been a normal lovers' quarrel. Later on, when Kathleen had had time to think about what had happened, she was cross with herself and her violent reaction. She felt sorry that she had said some of the things she had said, and wondered if Colin might not have made a good and responsible husband, even if he didn't love her. She wondered if it would be worth her apologising to him, but then she considered the idea of loving a man who did not love her in return. The thought was too upsetting. So she vacillated between the different feelings for a long while, not revealing any of the exchange that had taken place that Sunday afternoon.

Two full weeks went by before Rose made comment to her son.

'You haven't been over to see Kathleen lately,' she observed. 'Is everything all right between you?'

'She doesn't want to see me any more.' Colin let the announcement out without any ceremony.

'What! What has happened? I thought Kathleen was madly in love with you. I heard her mother say so on more than one occasion.'

'She found out.' Colin expected that his mother would understand without him having to spell it out.

'Found out? You didn't tell her about Emily, I hope.'

'No! I didn't tell her anything. She just guessed.'

'Guessed that you were still in love with Emily Wallace?'

'How do you know that I'm in love with Emily Wallace?' Colin asked annoyed. 'I haven't ever said anything about her. I don't ever mention her name!'

'It's true though, isn't it?' Rose pressed.

'I don't know!' Colin was sullen. 'All I know is that I don't love Kathleen Miller, and now she knows it as well.'

'How did she take it?' Rose asked.

'Not well.'

'Did you apologise?'

'Look, Mum! I tried. I'm totally in the wrong. I should never have led her along like that. There's nothing I can do to make up for what I've done. I'm thoroughly miserable about it. Are you happy?'

'So, now the three of you are miserable.'

'Three?' Colin asked.

'Kathleen, you and Emily.'

'Well it is as it is. There's nothing I can do to change it.'

Rose had to agree that the situation was hopeless in many ways. She was sorry that Kathleen Miller had been dragged into a hopeless love triangle. She knew that the girl had every right to be furious, but knowing Kathleen, she suspected that she would sooner blame herself than hold it against Colin for too long.

***

Emily was breathless with wonder. Mrs Hodges had allowed her to stay and assist with the birthing of Lilly's baby, and Emily was so full of amazement at what she had witnessed, that she didn't quite know what to say. The miracle of childbirth had never seemed so real and awe-inspiring as it did at that moment.

'Get along with you, child!' Mrs Hodges' friendly voice broke into Emily's thoughts. 'There isn't much more you can do for Lilly now. You'd better get along home before it gets too dark for you.'

Emily nodded her assent, but before she turned to leave, she offered one more word to the new mother. 'Your baby is so beautiful,' Emily spoke with tears in her eyes. 'I have never felt so full of happiness in my whole life. Thank you for letting me stay with you.'

'You're welcome, Emily. And thank you for all of the help you've given me these last few weeks. You really have been wonderful.'

'Whose goin' ta help you while you get back on your feet?' Mrs Hodges asked, as the subject came up.

'Oh, please,' Emily immediately offered. 'Couldn't I come and work for you until you are well?'

'What about your aunt?' Lilly asked, concerned that Emily had pushed Lady Wallace beyond patience. 'I have family and friends who can come, you know.'

'Yes, but I would love to spend just a bit more time with that new baby.'

Both Lilly and Mrs Hodges laughed. 'You'd best have a word with Lady Wallace first,' Mrs Hodges advised. 'If she doesn't object, then I'm sure this new bairn could use a little extra fuss.'

Emily walked out into the gathering darkness, but she was too full of joy to notice any gloom. Being on hand to experience a miracle was something she was sure she would never have had the chance to do if she had still been in her father's house. That life was so far away and so undesirable at the moment. Emily had continued to serve Lilly, with renewed motives, and had discovered many things she would never have known, had she still been a respectable member of polished society.

Before she had come to Australia, she had never heard anyone even talk about a baby being born, let alone having witnessed such an event firsthand. She realised just how small-minded and lacking in experience she really had been, and was suddenly thankful for all the opportunities that she'd been given of late, even despite her crooked purpose originally.

'Emily, is that you?'

Emily was arrested in her walk by the familiar voice calling out of the darkness. 'Christine?' She answered tentatively.

'I heard that Lilly had taken to her bed. Has there been any word yet?'

'Yes!' Emily replied, happiness colouring her tone. 'She's had a boy.'

Christine emerged from the grey shadows so that Emily could fully see her, and the two began to talk about what Emily had seen.

'Well, I have some more news for you,' Christine eventually spoke what was on her mind.

'What?' Emily was half afraid that she would hear that the wedding would be tomorrow, or worse yet, had been today.

'It's all broken off.' Christine stood and waited for Emily's response, and when there was none, she went on. 'Colin isn't going to marry Kathleen Miller after all. What do you have to say about that?'

'Poor Kathleen!' Emily expressed the sentiment with a genuine heart. 'She must be heartbroken.'

'She told him she never wanted to see him again!' Christine wasn't feeling as delicate as Emily. 'I don't think they've spoken to each other since.'

'Christine!' Emily scolded. 'This is a terrible thing. Kathleen Miller is a wonderful girl. I know she loved your brother very much.'

'So did you!' Christine countered.

'Yes! And so I know just how upset she must be.'

'But don't you understand,' Christine spoke as if Emily were a halfwit. 'This may mean that he really loves you instead.'

'No! I'm sorry, Christine. I have learned my lesson. I have worked very hard the last few weeks to get over my infatuation, and I don't intend to be building myself up with false hopes again.'

'All right!' Christine shrugged her shoulders. 'But I thought you'd like to know.'

'Thank you,' Emily patted her friend's arm. 'I am tempted to feel happy, but I can't on Kathleen's account. It wouldn't be right.'

'You're probably right.' Christine agreed. 'Well, I'm just going to look in on Lilly. Colin would like to have come himself, but you know it's not a man thing. Ned will have to give him all the details some other time.'

Emily waved Christine off into the darkness that was now becoming quite thick. She was glad that she had travelled this road many times, and that it wasn't too far back to the Wallace Estate, because everything took on a lonely, frightening air at this time of night.

Because Emily was travelling only by starlight, and she was being careful not to have another accident, she took nearly an hour to get home. She knew that it was probably two or three hours past when she would normally have arrived home, but she was certain that her aunt would forgive her when she'd heard about the baby.

'Aunt Vera,' Emily called excitedly, the moment she had set foot in the entrance hall. 'Aunt Vera.'

Lady Vera was only seconds in responding, indicative of the fact that she had been on edge, waiting for her niece's return.

'I'm sorry I'm so late,' Emily began, breathless, 'but you'll never guess what's happened.'

'Emily, child,' Vera spoke in a strained, almost fearful tone.

'Mrs Hodges let me stay for the birthing. Mrs Miller had her baby today.' Emily spouted her news without waiting for breath. 'Can I go back to help again next week? They said I could if you didn't object.'

'Emily. We need to talk.'

Emily suddenly became aware that something was seriously wrong. Lady Vera was often cross and disapproving, but this fearful tension was something Emily had never seen before.

'Aunt Vera. What's the matter?'

But before either one of them had a chance to go on, Emily was arrested by the sound of a voice – a voice from the past; a voice that made shivers run up and down her spine.

'What in god's name is going on here?' Lord Derickson stepped into the hall. 'What is the meaning of this?' He waved his hand up and down, indicating Emily's less than formal attire; the brown dress that had every stain of the day's work on it.

'Good god, woman!' Derickson spluttered angrily at Lady Wallace. 'You were supposed to be looking after her, not sending her out to work in some brothel.'

'I haven't been working in a brothel,' Emily defended.

'Shut your mouth!' Emily was instantly intimidated by this man's cruel air of authority. 'It might have been expected,' he went on. 'I should have known that since you couldn't survive in decent society, that you would drag your niece down to this.' Once again he held his hand out in a gesture of disgust, and his lip curled in a derogatory snarl.

'I have not been dragged anywhere. Aunt Vera has been very kind to me.' Emily couldn't stand by and see this man accuse her aunt of lies. But she didn't expect the retaliation that came. Lord Derickson stepped forward and brought a strong armed slap across her face, causing Emily to fall backward to the ground. 'You will learn to respect me,' he growled. 'Now get up off that floor and go to your room. I don't want to see you until you are dressed respectably. And wear something suitable for a wedding. We are going to be married just as soon as the minister gets here.'

'No! Not tonight!' Vera objected.

'Shut up, old woman.' Derickson was ruthless. 'Tonight we will be married, just to make sure she is mine, and tomorrow, we will get on our way back to England.'

'I won't marry you,' Emily shouted, stepping back from his reach. 'My father wouldn't make me if I didn't agree.'

'Your father is dead!' Lord Derickson seemed to gain delight by throwing the announcement out as if it didn't matter at all. 'As far as I'm concerned, I need you if I'm to get out of my debts.'

'But the Earl's estate has been willed to Charles,' Vera argued. 'What use is Emily to you?'

'She has money of her own. Not only has her father put aside a rather large dowry, but her mother's fortune went to her as well, and now it will go to me. Look!' He stepped forward in a threatening way again, taking hold of Emily's arm and yanking her forward. 'I wouldn't give two farthings for you, girl, but I need your money. And who knows, I might enjoy you yet if you keep fighting me like this. Now get up those stairs and make yourself ready to be a bride. I want this over and done with tonight.'

'I won't marry you, not ever!' Emily screamed, struggling to get out of his grasp.

Lord Derickson didn't bother to argue with her, only raised his hand and struck her harder than he had the first time, with the back of his fist. This time, Emily felt herself black out from the blow.

'You'll kill her,' Vera shouted. 'What use will her money be to you if she's dead? It won't go to you.'

'Then get her up stairs and get her ready before I do kill her.'

Vera stepped forward. For the first time in her life she was terrified. She had never seen such violence in a man before. Not ever. A dozen thoughts rushed through her mind as she helped Emily up from the floor and began to assist her up the stairs, not the least of which was how she was going to get her to escape.

'Father is dead,' Emily sobbed as her aunt tried to help her out of her dress.

'I'm sorry, child,' Vera was genuinely sorry, and nearly to the point of desperate, a state that she had not been in for many, many years.

'I can't marry him,' Emily's thoughts were still a little dazed. But her head was clearing from the blow. Vera could see a large purple bruise beginning to gather on the right side of her face, and her lip was swollen from a cut, resulting from the first hit.

'Listen, child,' Vera whispered. 'You've got to get away from here.'

'I'm afraid,' Emily replied, all of her bravado lost following the second attack.

'I'll help you get out the back way, and you'll have to make your way on your own.'

'Where should I go?' Emily asked, sounding just like a little girl. 'Won't the reverend make me come back here, if I go to them?'

'I doubt that he would, child,' Vera answered, 'but don't go there. I think that would be the first place Lord Derickson would look; and don't go to the Hodges' either. He has got Hodges on standby to bring Reverend Laslett here and to take you both away when you are married. I think you should go straight to the Shores'.'

'But . . . ' Emily didn't want to object, but it was such a long way, especially in the dark.

'Mr Shore is a reliable and honest man. He has already proven himself to us. You can trust him, I know. And his mother will take good care of you.'

'But what should I tell them?' Emily seemed helpless to think for herself.

'Tell them that you are not to move from there until I have sent word.'

'But what about you? Lord Derickson will hurt you if you don't tell him where I am.'

'I will be all right. It's you I'm worried about for the moment.'

Emily had nothing left with which to argue. She was afraid and hurting physically, and at that moment willing to do whatever her aunt told her to do. Just before she went through the back door into the dark night, Emily turned to her aunt with one more thing to say. 'I think you should know, Aunt Vera. Mr Shore is not going to marry that other girl after all.'

'Then God bless him, is all I can say,' Vera muttered. 'Now hurry, and be careful, child.'

Most of the family had retired for the night, but Colin was left alone on the front veranda – alone with his thoughts. He had been troubled by all that had gone on, and he had mentally punished himself over and over. Here he was again, sitting up late into the night, worrying over the little things that could not be changed. He had prayed often, but had felt that he was a hypocrite. If he had listened to God's voice in the first place, instead of taking matters into his own hands, he would not have hurt Kathleen so badly. He muttered yet another prayer under his breath, still hopeful that God might forgive him.

And then it happened. One moment he was haggling with his maker over past issues and what was to be done about them, and the next minute he was fully alert and prepared to take on an intruder.

'Who's there?' he called into the night. The animals had stirred, and he knew that someone was lurking about. He got up from his seat and took hold of the rifle that he had leaned up against the wall of the house. Pointing the gun into the darkness he called out again. 'Who's out there?'

He didn't quite know what happened next. It happened so quickly that afterwards he could not have said what was or was not said. All that he knew was that suddenly, he was holding Emily Wallace in his arms, and she was shaking and crying hysterically. As if it was a reflex, he swept her off the ground, and carried her up the steps, into the house, calling for his mother as he did so.

'What has happened, Emily?' Rose asked, the instant she came into the room and saw her young friend. But Emily still couldn't answer. By this time, Julianne and the other girls had joined them, and a lamp had been lit. When Colin saw the bruise and the cut on Emily's face, all of the protective love, and the accompanying fury came to the surface.

'Emily,' he spoke firmly to her, taking a strong hold of her shoulders. 'Tell me what has happened.'

'My father is dead.' She managed to get this much out, but it was not enough to satisfy Colin.

'How did you hurt yourself? Did you fall over in the dark?'

Emily shook her head, and hid her face in her hands.

'Who did this to you?' Colin demanded.

'Take it easy, son,' Rose spoke in a much more controlled tone. 'Let me talk to her.' The concerned mother knelt down next to Emily and, taking her hand away from her face, she began to probe for information. 'Has somebody hit you, Emily?' she asked gently. Emily nodded. 'Is it somebody we know?' To this question, she shook her head, and renewed emotion welled up.

'It's not that Derickson fellow?' Colin growled. He remembered the name as surely as he remembered his past crimes, though he had confused the son for the father. Emily confirmed that it was just as Colin had guessed, and even Rose could not believe the reaction that her son gave.

'I'm going to kill him,' Colin shouted as he pushed a chair back and began searching for his gun. 'He's done this before, and this time he will pay for it.'

'No!' Emily objected. 'Please, this is the other one. The father. He only hit me. this time.'

'Only!' Colin exploded. 'Do you think that makes any difference to me?'

'Think for a moment, son,' Rose cautioned. 'You don't know the full story yet, and seeing you in this fury, I could believe you would kill somebody, and then be hung for it.'

'Please, no!' Rose's words frightened Emily. 'Don't kill anybody, Colin. Please.'

Colin subdued just slightly, but he was still wound up like a tightly coiled spring.

'This man, Derickson, he has just come from England?' Rose prompted. Emily nodded. 'And he has come with news that your father has passed away?'

'Yes!' Emily allowed tears to fall, as she considered this dreadful news again. There were so many things that had not been said, and now she was not going to ever have the chance.

'What was it that made this man hit you?' Rose asked gently.

'He wants me to marry him – tonight.'

'And you refused?' Colin could not keep quiet listening to this exchange.

'What about your aunt? Does she want you to marry Derickson?' Rose continued.

'No! She helped me to get away. She told me to come here, but I'm afraid that he will hurt her too. He is an evil man.'

'That's it,' Colin stated firmly. 'I'm going to get to the bottom of this.' He turned to his mother to give his instruction. 'After you take care of those bruises, put her to bed in my bed. And don't let her leave this house until I come back.'

'Are you sure you know what you're doing?' Rose asked, half afraid, half proud of her son.

'I have no idea. But I'm not going to stay here and let a tyrant loose to beat any woman he feels inclined to beat.'

'Be careful, son,' Rose spoke the parting words. 'I'll look after Emily, but you make sure you look after yourself.'

CHAPTER 12

᠅❧

*L*ady Vera had managed to stave off Lord Derickson's demands for nearly an hour. 'The child is upset about her father,' she had made the excuse. 'Let her alone to grieve in private.'

'I don't care about her father. He was a spineless creature anyway.' Lord Derickson's words had begun to slur as the copious amounts of alcohol he'd drunk began to take effect. 'If she'd been my daughter, I would have made her marry when the opportunity first came up. Now I've had to waste all this time waiting for him to die.'

'You are not her legal guardian, sir,' Vera bravely attempted to reason with him.

'Her brother has given me leave to do with her as I wish.'

'Yes, but at the moment, I am responsible for her.'

Lord Derickson laughed an evil kind of laugh. 'How do you think you will stop me, old woman?' he mocked.

All of the insult that Lady Vera felt at these words were lost in the greater emotion of fear. Even though she knew that Emily was somewhere out in the night, Vera wondered if she really had any power to stop this wicked man from having his own way. She shuddered at the thought.

'Go up stairs and bring the little slut down here. I want to look at her.'

Anger and rebellion nearly consumed Lady Vera as she heard this man's vile language, but for the first time in her life, she didn't have the courage to challenge him to his face. Instead, she went through the pretence of going to Emily's room. She hoped that Reverend Laslett would not be long in coming. She had seen that gentleman take a firm stand on more than one occasion, and hoped that now he would be able to bring some control back into her house.

'Well? Where is she? I told you I want her down here now.' Derickson's impatience was even greater when he was drunk, and Vera wisely chose to stay well away from him.

'There is no point in dragging her down here before the minister arrives.' Vera hoped that he would accept the excuse.

'She will come down if I say she will. If you don't get her now, I will come up there and drag her down myself.'

Vera was nearly intimidated into going through the farce again, but instead was relieved to hear Alice showing Reverend Laslett into the drawing room.

'What's wrong, Lady Vera?' John asked, the moment he'd come through the door. 'Hodges said that it was urgent.'

'Are you the minister?' Derickson rudely interrupted.

'I am,' John answered, instantly aware that this man was the problem. 'Whom do I have the pleasure of meeting?'

'That's no concern of yours. Just get yourself ready. There's going to be a wedding, and you're going to conduct it.'

'I have no intention of doing anything of the kind, especially at this time of the night.' John was already inflamed and ready for battle, an attitude that brought great relief to the lady of the house.

'Who is this upstart?' Derickson almost accused Lady Vera. 'Tell him to do his duty.'

'Reverend Laslett is a man of conscience before God,' Lady Vera excused. 'He rarely does just as he's told, at least not until he is sure that it is right.'

'Then get me another minister.'

'Excuse me, sir,' John broke in, 'I don't know who you think you are, but you do not come into this lady's home and speak to her as you have just done under any circumstances.'

'I do not believe that I asked for your opinion. You may go.' Derickson still held onto the belief that he was superior in every way.

'No, sir. It is you who may go. Lady Wallace is not accustomed to being insulted in her own home in this way. I will not stand here and allow you to do it.'

'You are acting way above yourself, man,' Derickson threatened. 'If you must know, Lady Wallace, as she calls herself, has been looking after my future wife. I have come to collect her, and since you will not marry us properly, I will dispense with the ceremony, and take the girl anyway. Will that suit you?'

'To whom are you referring?' John felt the fear that had come upon the house.

'Are you going to perform the wedding, or will the girl have to go home in disgrace?'

John knew that this offensive man could be none other than the fellow Colin had told him about in reference to Emily Wallace. John had wondered about Colin's murderous thoughts of a few months ago, but now he was beginning to understand very clearly. He had just begun to formulate a plan of how he was going to forcefully prevent the crime that had been proposed, when the atmosphere was shattered by the sound of the door being violently thrown open. John didn't know whether to feel relieved or worried to see Colin Shore standing in the doorway, a loaded gun in his hand, and a look of fury clearly evident on his features.

'Is this the animal that has dared lay a hand on Emily?' Colin's tone was full of rage.

'I beg your pardon,' Derickson mocked. 'Now we have the peasants on first name basis. I suppose you've let her sleep with them as well.'

Vera was shocked and more ashamed of her class than she had ever thought she would be, but she was more afraid at the young man's reaction as it came.

Colin stepped forward with passion burning in his eyes; an obvious intention in his stance.

'Col,' John intervened. 'Think for a moment, friend. Killing him is not worth your own life. Let's deal with this rationally,'

Colin heard his counsellor's voice, and though he tossed the gun to one side, he was still determined to take physical action. 'Do you know what this monster has done to our Emily?' he asked, while he grabbed hold of the visitor's shirt front and shoved him up against the wall.

'He hit her,' Vera offered, hoping to diffuse the situation without shedding any blood. 'He hit her hard. Twice.'

'Is that all?' Colin demanded.

'He intended more,' John added, thinking of what he'd heard.

Derickson was full of false bravado, and, in the face of such opposition, stupidity. 'I'll do that and more if I want to,' he boasted. 'She is my property, after all!'

The little restraint that Colin had left suddenly disappeared, and he found himself bringing his arm back, aiming to strike Derickson's arrogant mouth; but John caught his hand, just in time.

'He is not worth your effort, Col,' John advised.

'What! You think we should just let him get away with all this . . . this . . . . '

'No! I won't. Neither will Lady Vera or yourself. We will see to it that this person is escorted from Green Valley, and we will make sure that Miss Wallace is properly looked after. You know that, don't you?'

Colin still had firm grip of Derickson's shirt and, though he was reluctant, he gradually let the large man down. 'If I catch you anywhere near her again, so help me . . . . '

'The woman you so bravely defend is to be my wife,' Derickson brushed at imaginary dirt. 'You can threaten me all you want. I will take what is mine.'

John held a restraining hand against Colin's tensed body. 'You make loud claims, sir,' John spoke firmly. 'I am yet to see any evidence that what you say is correct.'

'As I said before, you are acting far above yourself. And as for this peasant, I don't have to answer to him, or to any of you.'

'Yes, but you have to answer to me,' Lady Vera had regained an amount of confidence, seeing the protection that the two younger men offered. 'Earl Stanford Wallace, my brother-in-law, gave me written instructions to see to my niece's welfare while she was here in this country. I am her legal guardian here, and I do not give you permission to so much as speak her name. You are a disgusting and shameful man, and I would never allow my niece to be touched by you again. These young gentlemen have shown far more honour and courage than you have even made claim to.'

'I have the new Earl's permission,' Derickson boasted. 'As I said, he doesn't care what I do to his sister.'

'The lady is still in Australia, and I have had no written communication from her father to say that my duty has ceased. Her brother has no right over her. As far as I'm concerned, if my brother-in-law is dead, then his last letter to me will stand for eternity. Is that clear to you?'

'If you are going to be difficult, I will get new written authority from the young Earl. It will take a little extra time, but I will return and still claim what is rightfully mine.'

'We will see!' Lady Wallace dismissed this claim as invalid. 'In the meantime, I suppose I am obliged to offer you a bed for the night, but come first light, I want you out of my house, and out of Green Valley.'

'Is Miss Wallace safe with this man under your roof?' John asked, not fully aware of all that had gone on.

'Miss Wallace is totally safe,' Colin spoke in a low voice. 'My mother is looking after her for the moment.'

'Do you mean to tell me, she is not even in the house?' Derickson exploded.

'As I said before, this is no concern of yours. My niece's welfare is my responsibility.' Lady Wallace pretended she was tired of his constant argument.

Despite Derickson's drunken state, he could see that he had been temporarily outdone. He nodded his head in a fashion that would resemble a nobleman, and backed cautiously from the room.

'I don't trust him,' Colin spoke the moment Derickson had closed the door.

'Is Emily all right?' Lady Wallace was immediately reduced from her act of authority to her real state of worry. 'Did she make it to you all right?'

'Yes!' Colin answered. 'She made it to us, but I was not happy with the way she looked.'

'Will she recover?' Both John and Colin were amazed to see the genuine care and concern being expressed by Emily's aunt.

'I can't say,' Colin admitted. 'I tore out of there the moment I understood what was going on here. But I'm sure my mother will take good care of her for the time being.'

'I was so afraid,' Vera admitted, showing a vulnerability that John had never witnessed in all of his years in this parish. 'I don't trust this man either, Reverend. I'm scared he will hang about waiting for an opportunity to abduct Emily. I cannot think what ever possessed the Earl to think this Derickson was a worthy husband for his daughter. Thank goodness she is here with us, and not back at his mercy.'

'We must send Hodges to take him back to Brinsford,' John suggested.

'I will go with him,' Colin offered. 'I'm not going to let Miss Emily come back here until I'm sure this man is well and truly out of the district.'

Lady Vera looked at Colin, perhaps for the first time in her life. No longer did she see an inferior tenant farmer, not worth her attention. Suddenly, she saw a man she greatly respected, and to whom she felt greatly indebted. 'I don't quite know what to say to you, Mr Shore,' she spoke humbly. 'If it had not been for your open and honest dealings with us, I fear my niece might have been in terrible danger by now. And this is not the first time you have given us aid. We owe you a lot.'

John didn't know what to think seeing this miracle take place. He never imagined that he would ever see Lady Wallace openly admitting her gratitude, especially to someone she had always seen as her inferior. Still he was seeing it, and despite the circumstances, he couldn't help but offer a prayer of thanks to God for the change.

It had been a long night, full of tension. Colin had offered to stay on at the Wallace mansion, because, as they had all admitted, none of them felt that Derickson was to be trusted. Strangely enough, Lady Wallace had offered the young bodyguard the room next to Derickson's, which happened to be Emily's. It seemed an odd coincidence to know that as he occupied her room, she would now be fast asleep in his. But Colin could not sleep in her bed. Firstly, he could not bring himself to take comfort in a place where she usually lay. It would have been yielding to a temptation that was beyond his reach, if he had given way. But secondly, Colin could not allow his mind to submit to the deep rest that came with sleep. He was constantly alert to any sound that might have come from the adjoining room, scared that Derickson might still escape the house unnoticed, and somehow find out where Emily was.

And so, the sun had scarcely come above the horizon when Hodges set the team into motion, pulling the vehicle that transported Derickson and a very watchful Colin Shore away from Green Valley. There were no pleasantries offered between the men, and during the whole two-hour journey, hardly a word was spoken. Only as they neared Brinsford did Colin finally speak.

'I mean what I say, Derickson,' Colin growled. 'Don't let me catch you near Miss Wallace again, or I won't be responsible for my actions.'

'You are very cocksure of yourself, peasant,' Derickson spat. 'You might have threats, but it would pay for you to remember that I have influence and power. Nobody is going to take the word of some dirty farmer over the word of a respectable gentleman.'

'Respectable!' Colin almost choked. 'You will have to put on a better act than the one we saw last night.'

'I can act, when necessary. I think it is you who had better watch your back.'

Colin didn't take the threat seriously. By the time Hodges had let Derickson out at the train station, Colin was quite ready to wipe the whole incident from his mind. Derickson could have nothing more to use against Miss Wallace, he felt, and he was determined that he would watch her closely to make sure.

'I don't like the sound of things,' Hodges commented dryly as he and Colin drove away from Brinsford.

'Derickson is a coward,' Colin brushed the concern aside. 'He's full of boasts, but I don't think he'd be man enough to do anything against another man.'

'I hope you're right, son.' Hodges didn't sound confident. 'There are other things a powerful gentleman can do without fronting up to you, face to face, so to speak.'

The two travelled on for some time, a sombre mood having settled upon them both. Colin wanted to put the ugly situation behind them, and move back to some sort of normality. This incident had stirred again all of the passion and desire that had haunted him over past months. The episode with Kathleen Miller had temporarily taken his mind off of his innermost feelings, but that distraction was now far from his thoughts. He was consumed with thoughts of Emily Wallace. And yet, his old set of logic still refused to give him any peace. He still couldn't find a way that would bring satisfaction to his longings. It didn't matter how much he had done for her, or how much he wanted to do more, there was this huge chasm of social difference that persisted.

Hodges was unaware of the younger man's inner turmoil, but was stewing over his own thoughts. He had seen men like Derickson before. They were arrogant and proud, and quite capable of creating situations and circumstances that served their own selfish purposes. Just because Derickson had met a little opposition, Hodges felt, was no sure guarantee that he would simply leave Lady Wallace and her niece alone. Hodges was troubled, and still quite alert to the danger.

But even he, in this wisdom, did not foresee just how soon Derickson would act.

The buggy, in which the pair travelled, was no more than an hour out of Brinsford, moving at an easy pace, when it was approached and eventually overtaken by a group of horsemen.

At first Hodges didn't comprehend just who it was, but when they pulled around in front of his team, he began to recognise what was going on. Seven mounted troopers surrounded the one horse-drawn vehicle, and the captain in the group shouted out his instructions.

'We believe that one of you is a Mr Colin Shore. Is that correct?'

'Yes!' Colin answered, his bewilderment turning to an angry frustration.

'Colin Shore, we are placing you under arrest, in the name of her majesty.'

'What?' Colin could not contain his reaction. 'What for?'

Even as the captain read out the list of charges, three troopers dismounted and came across to the buggy, pulling Colin roughly to the ground.

'You are charged with assault, attempted murder, and kidnapping.'

'Now, just wait a minute,' Hodges sought to intervene. 'There's been some kind of mistake.'

'Who's made these accusations?' Colin pushed the question out, as his arms were aggressively pulled behind his back and secured in steel cuffs.

'You will have a chance to defend yourself before the magistrate,' the captain answered, apparently unconvinced and unconcerned that any miscarriage of justice was taking place.

Colin was not appeased by this small consolation, and he twisted his shoulders in a supreme effort to break free of his captors. This action was not calculated, other than a frustrated response to being falsely arrested; yet it brought about a violent reaction from the trooper nearest him. Though not as tall as the prisoner, the trooper easily had the advantage, with Colin being restrained, and he threw several hard punches, including a sharp blow across Colin's jaw. It left Colin winded, and with a bleeding lip.

'Steady there, boy,' Hodges advised. 'Go along quietly for now. I'll get back to the Valley and bring the reverend along as soon as possible.'

Hodges was as good as his word, and didn't waste another second pulling his rig away from the group, whipping the horses into a fast gallop. This left Colin alone with his captors. The captain was the sort of man who relished his position and the power it gave him, and he liked to take every opportunity to exhibit his authority.

'Seems like you'll need to have that fight knocked out of you, boy,' he sneered. 'He can run back to Brinsford.'

To Colin's horror, his hands were released then re-cuffed in front of him, and a rope attached so that he could be led along behind one of the horses. Apart from the pure exhaustion that would result from such a run, Colin felt the humiliation of being treated like a common criminal. As he began to pick up his feet to stop himself from being knocked over and dragged along the ground, Colin began to realise just who was behind this whole experience. He had not grasped what Hodges had said with regard to influence when mixed with arrogance.

Now it had hit him full in the face, and he was powerless to stop it from happening.

The captain was ruthless in the pace he set, and Colin's lungs soon burned from the harsh breath that he drew in and out. He must have run two or three miles at an unreasonable rate before his whole body resisted moving any more. His legs simply gave way, and he found himself being dragged along the dusty road, rocks and gravel scraping skin from his side, where his shirt had torn.

Just before he lost consciousness, Colin wondered if anybody from the Valley would really care about his predicament. He knew that they would all rush to Emily's aid, if she were in danger, but he somehow doubted that Lady Wallace would condescend to offering a defence on his behalf. He was, after all, only a lowly farmer.

CHAPTER 13

H odges drove the pair of horses at a frightening speed. He had no illusions about what had taken place. He knew that this was no mistake, rather a deviously planned scheme to get revenge on Colin Shore, which would also leave Lady Wallace and young Lady Emily with one less protector; the most valuable protector they had.

When he finally entered the Valley, he drove right by the entrance to the Wallace estate, and directly to the manse. First and foremost he wanted the advice of the minister. Reverend John Laslett was a man of action and a man of prayer, and at this point, Hodges knew that they would need both.

From the moment that Hodges had retold the horrible news, John moved into immediate action. He, like Colin, still had some doubt as to whether Lady Wallace would be prepared to go out of her way to help someone so inferior, but he had hope following the miraculous exchange he'd witnessed the night before. John hurried away from the manse, begging Kate to pray for their friends, and assuring her that he would be all right, even if he didn't return for several days. Kate had little choice but to take courage and do as he asked her.

From there, Hodges drove John to the Shore farm. There they informed Rose of what had taken place, and began to make arrangements for her to join them on their way back to Brinsford. The news upset the entire household.

'But what did he do?' Samantha cried, distressed to hear of her brother's arrest. 'He wouldn't hurt anybody.'

'It's not so much what he has done, Samantha,' John tried to explain. 'It's more a case of whom he has offended.'

'I don't understand,' June joined in, perhaps less expressive in her emotions, but no less worried.

'There isn't any time to explain now,' Rose spoke firmly. 'We must get to Colin straight away.'

'But what about Emily?' Christine asked.

'She is back with Lady Wallace, isn't she?' John asked, having not thought of her yet.

'No! Colin told us to keep her here until he sent word. We haven't heard if it's safe to send her home yet.'

'Where is she?' Hodges asked, already aware that she was not numbered amongst the rest of the Shore family.

'She and Julianne have gone for a walk,' Christine offered. 'They shouldn't be too far away. Mum warned them to stay close to the house.'

'Then we will take Miss Emily with us.' John spoke with authority, not revealing his fear that Derickson might even yet have stolen back in search of the unprotected young lady.

Finding Emily and trying to tell her the facts without alarming her too much proved to be a complex exercise. Emily had been very much affected by the appearance and cruel treatment of Lord Derickson. It had brought back a flood of memories from similar encounters of several years before, and the carefully constructed wall of confidence that she had hidden behind ever since coming to Green Valley, had simply crumbled. All that was left was a terror that was not easily calmed.

Eventually, it was Rose's tender understanding and mothering that brought some sense of peace to the situation. Rose thought she knew what Emily must have been feeling to some extent. She recalled the brutality of Samuel Jones, when he had tried to force himself upon herself and her family, and the fear that had followed the incident.

'It's all right, Emily,' Rose reassured. 'I will be with you all the way, and Reverend Laslett and Mr Hodges will be with us too. We won't let anything happen to you.'

Emily had complied, though her apprehension was still evident. 'It's all my fault that this has happened,' she mourned, just before they reached her home. 'I have brought all of this trouble on your son.'

'You can't blame yourself, Emily,' Rose contradicted. 'Colin has chosen to defend you and your aunt. Together, we must have the faith that God will bring good out of this situation.'

'But what good can come out of this? What if he is taken off to a prison somewhere? I don't want that to happen, Mrs Shore.'

'Neither do I, honey. Neither do I.'

***

Any doubt that John or Colin might have had about Lady Wallace's willingness to help was quickly blown away in a wild expression of outrage.

'That man is a disgrace to his country and his position!' she snorted, immediately moving towards the entrance hall. 'Have my things put in a trunk,' she barked this order to her maid. 'Is Hodges getting the carriage out?' she asked her butler. 'Oh, and please have some of Miss Emily's things prepared as well. We will be setting off in half an hour.'

'Then you will come?' John had to clarify what he was seeing.

'The young man is innocent of any charges. Do you think I am going to sit here and see him wrongly accused?'

'I had hoped that you would bring your testimony forward. Mr Shore is possibly without friends at the moment. And as you well know, he doesn't have any wealth to recommend him.'

'Fiddle-faddle. This business of judging a man because of what he owns, or because of the way he looks is outrageous. It has got to be stopped.'

If the situation hadn't been so serious, John felt he could have burst out laughing. The change in Lady Vera's thinking was so dramatic that he found it difficult to believe. He watched astounded, as this woman who had so opposed his marrying Kate because she was associated with her father's misdemeanours, and had been positively cold to Colin when he had saved Emily's life, now speaking as if she believed in human rights, and had done all along.

Colin had regained consciousness not long after he had lost it. He had lost only enough time for the troopers to throw his bruised body over the back of one of their horses, and tie him, hand and foot, like a sack of grain. The blood rushed painfully to his head, but he was reluctant to complain, as he thought it just as likely that he would end up being dragged again. Though uncomfortable, he was not going to be cut up any more, and his legs would not have to support him any more. He elected to close his eyes against the pain and wait until they had arrived at their destination. He hoped that it wasn't going to be too much further.

'So, what have you done to raise the captain's ire?' Colin turned his head on his bunk to see the familiar face of Doctor Michaels. 'You look pretty messed up, boy. I wouldn't have taken you for a criminal.'

'I'm not!' The simple denial was forced out over a parched and raw throat. Colin already felt that he was developing a fever. He didn't attempt to rise for the doctor, or even turn towards him. His body was enveloped by pain, and every movement brought renewed bolts to remind him of his ordeal.

'Well, I suppose it will be up to the magistrate in the end,' Doctor Michaels commented, pulling a stool up close to the rough bed. 'I see I'm going to have a job getting you patched up. But you know how it is. They want you alive and well before they condemn you.'

Colin wanted to argue and defend himself, but he didn't have the strength. 'Water!' It was the only word he felt important enough to spend precious energy on.

It took the better part of two hours for Doctor Michaels to stitch closed several lacerations, to clean and dress numerous other cuts and scrapes, and eventually administer a powder he hoped would dull the young man's senses to the pain of the bruises. 'I hope that young lady of yours has some influence,' he commented before getting up to leave. 'If you've taken sides against some powerful aristocrat, you are going to want all the friends you can muster.'

The magistrate allowed only two days for Colin's fever to break, and for him to be able to at least stand before the bench. During that time, John had brought Colin's mother to the prison, but neither one had been allowed permission to enter. John had decided there and then that they would do all they could to prepare a defence.

'So! In the case of the crown versus Colin Charles Shore, the prosecutor maintains that Mr Shore has assaulted and caused bodily harm on two counts; has threatened with the intent to murder; and has abducted a minor.' The magistrate's voice held no interest as he read out the charges. 'How do you plead, Mr Shore? Guilty or not guilty?'

'Not guilty!' Colin spoke as calmly as his fury would allow him. He had been surprised to come to the court-room and find a professional lawyer ready to defend him. He wondered if Hodges had gotten the message to John, and if this learned man was now standing in his defence because of John's influence. He truly hoped so.

'Your worship,' the voice of the crown prosecutor addressed the magistrate, 'I would like to call the witness, Lord Richard Derickson, to the stand.'

'Very well.'

Colin watched with a feeling something akin to hatred as Derickson approached the witness stand. Unlike the previous time they had met, Derickson was now completely sober, his clothes and hair done impeccably, and he held himself with every ounce of grace and charm he could afford. Colin's defence lawyer had tried to impress upon him the importance of withholding any emotional outburst in front of the magistrate. It was a very difficult thing for him to listen to the arrogant lord spinning all sorts of lies about what had actually happened. All during the testimony, Colin had to remind himself continually not to burst out in rage, and he was successful for the most part, but when Derickson came to the last part of his fabricated story, Colin couldn't contain himself any longer.

'You see,' Lord Derickson had adopted a mournful tone, 'it was her father's dearest wish that I come and bring her back to her beloved homeland. Imagine my distress to find that she had been forced into service by her cruel and unfeeling aunt. Of course, I insisted that this horrible abuse had to stop straight away, and I believe that Lady Emily was relieved to find that at last someone had come to rescue her from the dreadful conditions she had been forced to live under.'

'What happened that night, after you had arrived, and informed Lady Wallace that she could no longer use your fiancée in such a way?' The prosecutor prompted the story along.

'Oh, I don't blame Lady Wallace. She is only one woman alone out here, and didn't really understand just what this man was up to.'

'What exactly was this man, Mr Shore, up to?'

'He was using Lady Emily for his own purposes, if you understand what I mean.'

'That's a lie!' Colin was on his feet, despite the pain it brought, and shouting at the witness. But his efforts were not applauded. Instead, he was given a stern warning that if he could not control his outbursts he would be removed from the courtroom, and the trial would proceed without him. In the meantime, Lord Derickson sat smugly on the witness stand, and produced a look of genuine sympathy as he continued.

'You should have seen poor Lady Emily. The way they dressed her was appalling, and then, this man, Mr Shore, came storming into the house. He threatened me with a gun, and dragged Lady Emily away with him.'

'Is that all you saw?' the prosecutor asked.

'I saw him hit her across the face twice. She was bleeding and crying, but he dragged her away just the same. There was little I could do.'

'Did you try to save Lady Emily?'

'She is my fiancée. Of course I tried.'

'And what happened when you did?'

'He had her thrown into the back of his wagon, before I approached him outside. When I came upon him, I demanded that he release Lady Emily. He didn't have his gun at this point, and so I felt I could easily defeat him, but he is a powerful young man. He managed to throw several well aimed punches, and I found myself on the ground, with him driving away with my lady.'

'What did you do then?'

'I hurried into Lady Wallace to ask where we could find troopers.'

'She insisted that it was too dangerous to go after them in the dark, and so we waited until morning. But somewhere along the way, she must have felt the threats of Mr Shore, because in the morning, she demanded that I come here, to Brinsford. You must imagine my surprise when I found out that Mr Shore intended to see that I was thrown out of Green Valley himself. He kept a gun on me the entire trip, and issued several more threats about returning. I have been worried sick about Lady Emily, and am only glad that this monster has been apprehended.'

Colin was thoroughly sickened and disheartened at what he had just heard, especially considering it was supposed to be the truth before God. He cast a searching look toward his defence, hoping to see some sign that all of this was just some terrific nightmare. But if the lawyer had any real defence, he did not indicate it by his expression.

There was only one other witness for the crown, and Colin sat amazed at how such men of influence could lie under oath.

'This Mr Shore not only resisted arrest, but tried to assault several of my men,' the captain said. 'He was like a wild man in his attempts to get away. In the end we were forced to take serious action to prevent him from killing any of us.'

By the time the magistrate had adjourned the court for the afternoon, Colin was thoroughly discouraged. The whole day had been spent listening to false accusations, followed by false testimonies. Bit by bit he began to wonder if the magistrate would simply accept the evidence as fact, and he would soon find himself on a chain gang somewhere, building another road for the developing colony.

John was thankful that he had at last been called to the witness stand. He had not had a chance to speak with his friend. This was apparently a precaution so as not to allow the prisoner time to corroborate his story. John had organised for Alexander Martin, the defence lawyer, to come all the way from Melbourne to defend Colin in this trial. The man had been recommended to him by Lady Wallace, and he understood that she also intended to pay the required fee. John had not had an opportunity to communicate this or any other information to Colin. Now, as he walked into the courtroom, he thought he saw relief in Colin's eyes. *He didn't even know I was here*, John thought to himself.

John went through the motions of swearing the oath, before revealing to the court who he was, and what position he occupied.

'Tell me, Reverend Laslett,' Alexander Martin began his examination, 'what was the course of events, as you saw them, on the night in question?'

John began to relay the story to the court, just as it had happened. He was unaware of the lies that Lord

Derickson had told, or of the way that his version conflicted so sharply.

The crown prosecutor was most eager to cross-examine the witness.

'Was Lady Emily actually performing the duties of a servant, Reverend Laslett?' he asked.

'Yes, but that was because . . . . '

'Just a simple yes or no will suffice.' He cut John off from his explanation.

'Did you see the defendant, Mr Colin Shore, take any physical action against Lord Derickson?'

'Yes, sir, but once again there were . . . '

'Please restrict your answers to what you are asked.'

'Did the defendant threaten Lord Derickson with a loaded gun?'

'Mr Shore had a gun, I don't know if it was loaded.' John didn't try to give more information, despite his frustration.

'Is it true that Mr Shore took Lady Emily to his home, and ordered her to stay there?'

'I could not say that it was the truth. I never saw him take her there, and I wasn't there to hear any such order.'

'Very well. Did you have occasion to pick up Lady Emily in the last couple of days?'

'Yes, sir.'

'Where did you find her?'

'She was staying with Mrs Shore, the defendant's mother.'

'Were there any signs of injury on Lady Emily's face?'

'Yes.'

'What was Lady Emily wearing at the time?'

'She wore a normal working dress.'

John could not have known that every answer he gave was confirming the lies that Lord Derickson had so carefully woven.

'Did Lady Wallace prevent Lord Derickson from going after Lady Emily on the night in question?'

'Of course.'

'And did the defendant, Mr Shore, accompany Lord Derickson out of the district?'

'I did not see them leave. I am unable to comment.'

'Thank you, Reverend. That will be all.'

Colin, who had heard all the testimonies, was horrified at the way the prosecutor had added credibility to Derickson's story, while at the same time throwing doubt on the minister's.

Hodges had been called to the stand and had given a similar account, based on the things he had seen, but once again, the prosecutor had managed to focus on the incriminating evidence.

'Did the defendant carry a gun with you on your journey here to Brinsford?'

'Yes, but . . . . '

'And did he threaten Lord Derickson at all?'

'Of course, but . . . . '

'Thank you, sir. That will be all.'

Colin was beginning to lose hope of ever hearing the truth. But then, a miracle happened. Colin had not really thought that she would, but she did. Lady Wallace, herself, appeared as the next witness. She boldly stepped up and swore the oath. She told her version of the story with confidence, not imagining for one moment that her reputation could ever be called into question. So when the prosecutor tried to twist her evidence to fit Derickson's tale, he was somewhat surprised.

'Now you see here,' Lady Wallace snapped at him. 'I have been known and respected in this district for the best part of thirty-five years. My husband and I have always been upright in our dealings, I have never lied and do not plan to do so now.'

'I am not asking you to lie,' the prosecutor patiently spoke. 'All I am asking you is if your niece has been working as a servant.'

'I will tell you the answer, and I will tell you the reasons for it, and I don't want any of your high and mighty interjections. If this court is interested in truth, then you had better hear it, because I am beginning to believe that somebody has poisoned your mind with something other than the gospel.'

The magistrate knew Lady Wallace's reputation, and was currently amused by her actions. He did not prevent her from continuing. Lady Vera began the whole story from the beginning again, not leaving out any of the less than proper details, and including the state of her own attitude as it had been toward Colin Shore.

'And so you see,' she began her conclusion, 'my niece, Lady Emily, has chosen the man she wants to marry. Though I did not approve at one stage, she was determined to win him. Following this unfortunate incident with this other person,' she waved her hand toward Derickson, 'I have come to value and respect Mr Colin Shore. He is honest and honourable, and I might just as well say, that when he feels he is ready, I will welcome him as my nephew-in-law.'

The magistrate felt he had heard enough evidence at this point and decided to ask a question of his own. 'It would appear that Lord Derickson has adjusted the story somewhat, Lady Wallace.'

'I should like to hear his version,' she sniffed. 'He is a worm of a man, and I have no respect for him whatsoever.'

'That may well be, madam, however he has made claims of authority in reference to your niece. Is it true that he has the young Earl's permission to marry Lady Emily, and return her to England?'

'I have seen no written authority, but I can produce the original letter written to me by my brother-in-law. As far as I'm concerned, I am yet to be convinced that this snake is even a member of the nobility. He has shown me no such proof that he is even who he says he is. I do wish you would arrest the right person.'

The magistrate sat back in his chair, and held his chin in his hand, in a thoughtful pose. 'If you can produce this letter, Lady Wallace, it would appear that you might have a case against this gentleman. On the other hand, he might be able to produce some written proof, as you have suggested.'

'So be it!' Lady Wallace seemed perfectly satisfied.

The magistrate leaned forward again. 'It is the will of this court that the said letter or letters be produced. Until that time Lord Derickson will be retained in custody.'

'Pardon me, your worship,' Alexander Martin sought his attention. 'What is to become of my client, Mr Colin Shore?'

'I do not see that any of his actions were more than any man would do for his wife if she were under attack. The evidence is clear, Mr Colin Shore is found innocent on all charges. He is free to go home.'

CHAPTER 14

*H*odges left Brinsford bound for Green Valley the
next day. Lady Wallace had asked that he return
to the mansion, and had given him instructions
of where to find Earl Stanford Wallace's letter. She had
decided that she would stay on in Brinsford until the
matter concerning Lord Richard Derickson was finally
settled. It was her hope that they would actually be able
to press charges of their own, and that he would be dealt
with by the same court that had sought to convict Colin
Shore.

'Take Lady Emily to the manse,' she instructed the
driver. 'Tell Mrs Laslett that her husband will stay on here
with me until we are sure that we are safe from this menace.'

'Would it be too much to ask that we convey Mr Shore
and his mother back to their home on this trip?' Hodges
asked this question on their behalf.

'Of course not,' Lady Wallace snapped as if it had been
her full intention. 'You will need to see if the poor fellow
is up to travelling. He looked rather the worse for wear
when I saw him yesterday.'

Though Colin was not really up to sitting in a carriage
for two or three hours, he didn't want to stay in Brinsford
for one moment longer than was necessary. In spite of his
mother's concern, he accepted Hodges' invitation to
return that morning.

Emily was a bundle of nerves, sitting on the seat
opposite the Shores. Her whole world was in turmoil, and

she didn't have the confidence to lift her gaze from her lap. She no longer had the ability to hide her tattered emotions behind a mask of carefree abandon. The incident involving Lord Derickson had not only terrified her, but had opened up the trauma concerning the other incident with his son, Frederick Derickson. Tangled with all of these painful memories was the knowledge of what she had tried to do to manipulate Colin Shore, and now she was aware of just what he had suffered on her account. She could not think of a single suitable thing to say to express her regret; she did not have the courage even to look up.

If she thought that Colin or Mrs Shore had found her behaviour strange in any way, she was wrong. Both Rose and her son were involved with their own set of worries, and had not thought beyond just getting themselves back home. Rose did not know the full extent of her son's injuries, but she knew him well enough to know that he was not well. She judged his state by his poor colour, and the look of pain in his eyes. However, there was little she could do for him, other than pray.

One of the hardest things she asked for from God was for him to give her forgiveness for the men who had done this to Colin. She had known all along that he was innocent of any crime, and though it was a relief to have the magistrate pronounce it, there was still the issue of this apparently unprovoked physical abuse. Colin did not want to talk about it, but she could not imagine that he had resisted the troopers to any serious degree, certainly not to the extent that they should do this to him. She sat quietly next to him, fully mindful of his condition, but respectful of his own wish to not discuss anything that had gone on. Rose knew that Emily, sitting opposite, was miserable, but she didn't have any words to heal her hurts.

And so the three passengers travelled in silence, jostled about by the carriage whenever it hit a rut in the road. Rose saw Colin's head droop and his eyelids gradually close, and hoped that he would be able to sleep. But it was hardly two minutes before the coach gave a great lurch because Hodges was unable to avoid a particularly large pothole. As Colin fell against the side of the coach, bolts of pain shot from his angry wounds. Both women were surprised to hear him issue a mild oath in his frustration.

'Col!' Rose didn't want to reprimand him, but she couldn't just let it go. 'Remember there are ladies present.'

'Sorry!' There was no real repentance in his apology.

'Why don't you lie down on the seat?' Rose suggested. 'I'll move over next to Emily.'

Colin nodded his head in agreement. 'I'm sorry,' he offered again, this time a little more gently. 'I haven't really slept for the past week.'

Rose got up and moved across the carriage. 'I hate to ask, dear,' she addressed Emily. 'Would you mind if we borrowed your cloak. If I roll it up, Colin could use it as a pillow.'

'Of course.' Emily was quick to co-operate. It was a small effort, but it was the least she could do, considering she felt totally responsible for his state.

Colin didn't acknowledge Emily's gesture, but accepted his mother's efforts as he would have in years gone by. This denial, though small, sent serious doubts spiralling through the young lady's mind. Quite suddenly, she wondered if Colin Shore blamed her as much as she blamed herself. The idea was quite alarming.

Several more miles were covered without incident. Rose began to relax seeing that Colin had finally fallen asleep, and she hoped that they would make it all the way back to Green Valley without further trouble. But a large rock on the road soon brought that hope to an end. The back wheel of the carriage hit the rock, sending the carriage careering on three wheels before landing with a heavy thump back on the road. The result inside was that Colin, who was fast asleep, was thrown forward off the seat into the waiting hands of the two women. This time, one oath didn't seem to cover the extent of the pain. No matter how offensive it was to his mother's ears, Colin was angry and frustrated and he felt as if one of his wounds had torn open.

'Colin! Please!' Rose spoke sternly. She felt sorry for him, but was disappointed to hear such coarse language come from his mouth.

'I'm sorry, Mother,' he turned an anguished eye toward her. 'As I said before, I can hardly think, let alone worry about what is proper and what is not.' He saw the look of disapproval in her eyes, and was somehow angered by it. 'Would you like to see what it is I have been cussing about?' He did not say this as a threat, more as a statement of his intent, as he began to unbutton his shirt.

'Colin!' Rose didn't know whether she should show him compassion or anger.

'I think one of them is bleeding again,' he justified his action, wincing as he struggled to get the shirt off. 'Can you see?'

Once the full extent of his injuries was laid open for Rose to see, she forgot about propriety, and began to inspect the many cuts and abrasions. She could see that Doctor Michaels had done his best to dress the wounds, but there was little he could do for the massive bruises that filled in all the gaps.

'Several of these stitches have split,' Rose commented. 'I will have to watch them, perhaps even stitch them again.'

She took her linen handkerchief and pressed gently, to stem the fresh bleeding. It didn't surprise her when Colin flinched at her touch. She could see the redness which showed infection. As carefully as she could, considering the unpredictable stability of the carriage, Rose tended the open wound before draping the shirt over his shoulders again. She did not insist that he put it on properly and do it up. The effort was more than necessary, and would only increase the discomfort he already was experiencing, and so, even though Rose was aware of Emily's stricken expression, she ruled in favour of common sense.

Emily was horrified by the whole scene. The very idea of seeing a man without a shirt was enough to cause her to panic, and she tried to hide her eyes at once. But Rose's heartfelt expressions of sympathy were enough to make her just a little curious. The moment she had stolen a glance, her eyes held. The sight before her made her stomach turn. When she had been injured, she had not had to look at the gash on her forehead. Now, her gaze was fixed upon a mass of cuts and bruises, some scabbed over, and some still red and weeping. Emily's head spun. She wanted very much to yield to the fashionable fainting spell that young ladies often employed when they could not, or would not face a situation. But try as she might, a faint seemed impossible; only a wave of nausea took its place. She was never more thankful to see the last of Colin Shore as she was when the carriage pulled up outside his house. Rose and Colin managed to get out without too much difficulty. Colin didn't stop or turn to say goodbye. He just limped slowly toward the house. Rose, still sensitive to Emily's state, did make an effort.

'I'm so sorry, Emily,' she apologised. 'Colin has always been disagreeable whenever he's unwell. He'll regain his spirits when he begins to heal properly.'

Emily nodded, tears shining in her eyes.

'You'll be all right with Kate,' Rose went on. 'It won't be long and everything will be back to normal.'

Once Hodges started the carriage under way again, Emily fell back on the leather seat and let her tears flow in earnest. At that moment, it seemed as if the whole world was in ruin.

Kate had not bothered to ask any questions when Hodges delivered Emily to her door. She allowed the young lady to go straight to the spare room, and though she knew that she was distraught, Kate wisely decided to let her work through the storm before trying to talk with her.

Hodges informed the minister's wife of what had happened with regard to the trial, and the journey back. He left her then, to go on with the task of retrieving the important letter.

Emily eventually fell asleep, and didn't wake up for the rest of the day. It wasn't until Kate had served dinner to her two young daughters that Emily shyly made her appearance in the dining room.

'Are you feeling better?' Kate asked kindly.

Emily nodded.

'Would you like something to eat?'

Emily shook her head to decline the offer. Though she did feel a little better than she had when she'd arrived, she still couldn't think of eating. Her emotions were too upset even to think of trying to keep any food down.

Kate hurried up her task of feeding the children, and then putting them to bed. She knew that it was finally time to talk, and while she wasn't prepared to neglect her children's needs, she didn't want to lose the opportunity.

It was nearing eight o'clock by the time Kate had at last settled the girls in their beds. She joined Emily in the parlour, bringing a tray of tea and cups with her.

'I thought you might like something to drink,' she suggested.

'I can't,' Emily refused the offer.

'You haven't eaten all day, dear.' Kate was a little worried about this fact.

'I just couldn't eat, Kate,' Emily explained sadly. 'I don't know if I'll ever be able to eat again, I feel so terrible.'

'Is it because of your father?' Kate decided to open up the issue.

'Yes! And all of the other things.'

'What other things?' Kate prompted.

Emily was apprehensive about sharing the experiences that were so terrible to her. She had never wanted to think about them again, let alone ever hear herself confessing that they had actually happened. Kate listened patiently, many times tempted to cry out her own disbelief and outrage. To hear of the things that Frederick Derickson had tried to do to this dear child made Kate's blood boil in fury. And she was no less affected to hear of Lord Derickson's cruel and abusive behaviour. Emily shed a good many tears as she spoke, and Kate allowed some of her own to flow in a sharing of the burden.

'I never thought I could trust a man again,' Emily confided. 'Even Charles seemed to be lustful. Oh, he never raised a hand against me, but I saw what he was doing behind our father's back. When I arrived in Australia, I had almost managed to block out all that fear and mistrust. I thought I could start again.'

'Many of us try to pretend that the past never existed,' Kate eventually spoke. 'It's our human way of denying the pain we feel inside.'

'But it wouldn't stay hidden.' Emily wanted to go on. 'That night, when Colin Shore found me on the hillside, I was full of fear and mistrust again. I thought that he was the same as Frederick Derickson, and that he meant to do just what Derickson tried.'

'But he didn't, did he?' Kate tried not to sound as if she had wondered about this.

'No! Colin Shore isn't like those other men. It was on that night that I fell in love with him. When he held me close, I felt safe and secure. I want to feel like that again. I want him to hold me close again. I want to feel safe, Kate.'

'I understand that,' Kate agreed. 'It's just that you might be placing more hope in him than is really fair.'

'But just the thought of him makes me feel safer. I just know that he would be able to bring me out of this terrible fear. If only he wasn't so angry with me.'

'What makes you think that Colin is angry with you?'

'He must be. How could he be anything else? I have brought him nothing but trouble ever since we met. Oh, it's all so hopeless. With him, I know I would have the chance to be happy and free, and yet I don't think I will ever have the opportunity again.'

'Emily,' Kate spoke sternly. 'I have to tell you something, and perhaps you are not going to like what I say, but you must listen and understand for your own good.'

Emily heard the sound of reprimand in her friend's tone, and she sat up just that little bit straighter.

'Your thinking is all wrong,' Kate began. 'Even if Colin Shore came to you, and wanted to marry you tomorrow, you would not find the peace you so desperately want. No husband in the world can give you what you really need.'

'What about your husband?' Emily asked, unwilling to accept her words. 'Reverend Laslett is a wonderful man. I can see that you are very happy.'

'Yes! We are both very happy, but it is not I who makes him truly happy, nor he, me. The true depth of our peace and security comes from our individual relationships with our Maker. As we have each sought to face issues and character flaws with the help of the Holy Spirit, we have found that our ability to love and relate to one another has increased over and over. Jesus Christ is the one who teaches us about selflessness, and about the real meaning of love. Without that, John and I would be as miserable as we were when we were first married.'

'I can't believe that,' Emily sounded doubtful. 'I've heard you talk about a relationship with Jesus before, but I don't see it like you do. Jesus is the man in the painting on the church wall. We hear the minister talk about him on Sundays, but I can't see what relevance he can have for me now.'

'And that's where your problem lies,' Kate declared confidently. 'Until you get beyond yourself, allow the Holy Spirit to challenge your selfishness, and give him a chance to heal your past hurts, any relationship between you and Colin Shore will only result in disappointment and more hurt. You must understand that, Emily.'

'I understand what you're saying,' Emily responded, 'but it all sounds too complicated. If only Colin Shore could love me the way I love him, then I know I would be all right.'

'You're wrong, Emily.' Kate had finished being diplomatic. 'What you call love for Colin is simply your own selfish desires. You don't want the best for him. You only want what will make you feel good.'

Emily didn't like hearing these words, and dropped her head and pouted.

'Colin doesn't need a wife whose entire purpose is continually to draw out of him what she needs, especially when he, being only human, cannot possibly heal your hurts, or bring you peace. I'm glad he is angry with you, Emily. You would both be miserable if you married at the moment!'

Emily hated the words that Kate had challenged her with. She didn't like the thought that she was being selfish, and she didn't like the idea of having to give up Colin Shore. She graciously excused herself, feigning tiredness, and went to the spare room to stew over what had been said.

But though she climbed into her bed, she could not get to sleep any more than she could erase the challenge from her mind. She tossed and turned for the entire night, Kate Laslett's words going on over and over in her head.

Colin hated the fact that he was forced to stay in bed for several days. He had tried on a number of occasions to get up and go about his normal work, but apart from the pain, there were several infections, and he had to admit to his mother that he was feverish. Rose fretted and fussed over him in a way that made him feel vulnerable. He hated that feeling. Colin had become used to being in control; always able to apply himself to any problem and usually to see some solution.

Now he was flat on his back. Some of his minor scrapes were healing well, and the bruising was less tender than it had been, but two of the larger wounds had become infected, and it was the effect of the fever that kept him off his feet more than anything else. He could see the concern in his mother's eyes, but knew there was nothing any of them could do to help. Either he would get better on his own, or he wouldn't. Even if they could have afforded to call Doctor Michaels out, all the way from Brinsford, Colin was not sure that there was much he could do.

And so the situation descended as a cloud of worry over the small farmhouse. Julianne and Christine didn't even grumble about having to shoulder all of the outside work. The whole family prayed for their brother's full recovery and took on a completely new air of sensitivity and compassion. When Rose was looking for something to thank God for, she found this fact to be high on the list, despite the seriousness of their circumstances.

Colin had several lapses into delirium. It was while he was below the surface of consciousness that he was faced with an alarming thought. What if Derickson came back to Green Valley while he was as helpless as a baby? What if he found Emily and took her? What if Colin were not able to prevent him from hurting her again? Even in his dreams Colin felt the full weight of what it meant to be at someone else's mercy. Somewhere from the depths of his being, he cried out to God. In past years, he had held his faith in God as an added extra; for when all else failed. Colin had not consciously declared it, but he had believed that he was physically capable of dealing with any problem that might arise. He had felt that he could provide for his family; that he could protect Emily; that he could fulfil his father's vision. But this particular hallucination was enough to make him realise that God was his total source of strength. Now, more than ever, if he were going to ever succeed again, he had to acknowledge God, and yield to His superior strength.

When the fever finally broke, and Colin emerged from his unconsciousness, he found John Laslett sitting by his bedside. He didn't have to ask to know that his minister friend had been praying for him.

'I think God has spoken to me,' were Colin's first words. 'Perhaps I have been a bit too bull-headed.'

'Perhaps!' John was not going to rub salt into the wound, so to speak. 'I'm glad to see you alive. Didn't know if you would make it for a while.'

'Is Mum all right? Does she know I'm awake?'

'I'll go tell her. She's been very worried.'

'Thanks.' Colin was thirsty, and didn't have the physical energy to talk much.

Rose hurried into the sickroom. She had brought water with her, but was more intent upon expressing her relief. 'Son! I thought I'd lost you there for a while. Thank the Lord that he has healed you.' She was careful when she kissed his forehead. 'You have been such a blessing to me, since your father died. I don't know where I'd have been if I'd lost you too.'

Colin didn't have much to say in response. He was still very weak. 'How did things turn out in Brinsford?' He directed this question to John, who stood in the doorway.

'The magistrate was satisfied that Lady Wallace was Emily's legal guardian. He found Derickson guilty of assault, trespass and perjury.'

'What did he get?' Colin asked.

'I hope you won't be angry at this, Col, but the magistrate had him escorted to Port Melbourne, put in the custody of the ship's captain, and he was basically warned never to return to Australia again.'

'Is that all?' Colin was upset.

'Derickson is a very powerful man, Col, but at least we can know that if he does show his face here again, the magistrate has said that he will experience the full weight of the Queen's justice.'

There were a few moments when resentment burned in Colin's heart. Here he was, near death, suffering from injuries that had come because he had been falsely accused, while the real criminal had been graciously escorted to a waiting ship.

'Bitterness isn't going to hurt anyone but yourself.' It was as if John had read Colin's thoughts. 'Let's just be thankful that Derickson is no longer a threat to Miss Emily. Now we can all get back to our normal life.'

Colin didn't make any verbal response. What normal life was there? Even before Derickson had shown up, Colin had been in the grips of confusion. His emotions were at war with his logic and pride, and in the end, even Colin didn't know which was more likely to win.

Rose somehow sensed his mental torment, and decided to broach the subject. 'I heard about what Lady Wallace said at the trial, Col.'

'Which was . . . ?' Colin thought he knew exactly what his mother was referring to, but it was still something he had no clear thoughts on.

'You know, how she would welcome you as her nephew-in-law.'

The minister and the mother watched Colin's facial response closely and saw exactly what he felt – emotional turmoil.

'Do you intend to do anything about it?' Rose pushed gently.

'Like what?' Colin played dumb.

'Like telling Miss Emily how you feel. Giving her the chance to respond.'

'And how do I feel, Mother?' He didn't intend to be harsh, but his indecision had reduced his tolerance.

'I think you love her, son,' Rose pushed boldly. 'I think that you are completely in love with her.'

'And so you think I should rush out of here, ask her to marry me, and then what? I can bring her back here and she can squeeze in here beside me,' he patted the narrow bed on which he lay. 'Perhaps I might be able to afford some material for her to make a new work dress. That would be a grand thing for her, wouldn't it? And then, when Harry is fast asleep, we can share a few intimate moments together.' He finished with heavy sarcasm.

'I think you're being a little hard on your mother, Col,' John interjected. 'She sees the desire of your heart, and is trying to encourage you in it.'

'But she's offering me false hope. How long do you thing a rich young lady like Emily is going to be happy in a hovel like this? Even if Emily was stupid enough to accept me, it wouldn't be long and she would resent me for the rest of her life. Poverty isn't for the likes of Miss Emily Wallace. It's hopeless, John. I won't do it.'

Rose released a sigh of disappointment. She saw Colin's point, but felt sorry that it had to be that way.

'There's something else you don't understand, Col,' John pressed the issue, once Rose had gone out.

'I think I understand the situation very well.'

'No! You don't! Emily Wallace is a very rich young lady. Not only did she inherit her mother's fortune, but her father would have put aside a dowry. Every good English father does. That money is supposed to be yours, should you marry the daughter.'

Colin was silent for a few minutes, and John wondered if he had even heard him. But then, Colin spoke, and indicated the true depth of his pride.

'If you think that I'm going to marry a wife for her money, so that I can live off of what belongs to her, then you are seriously mistaken.'

'There are hundreds of English gentlemen who would not think twice about it, Colin. Look at how far Derickson was prepared to go to get Emily's money.'

'Exactly!' Colin felt that he had proved his point. 'Derickson and I are worlds apart, and I would not stoop to such an act. I do have some self-respect. When I marry, I will provide a home and see to the needs of my wife and children. I do not wish to become a charity case.'

'Colin, you are a responsible provider now. No one could ever doubt you on that. What you have done for your mother and sisters is a credit to you. I doubt that anyone would ever accuse you of chasing after Emily's money. All I'm saying is that she need not ever live in "poverty" as you call it. She will always have enough to preserve her standard of living, if she really wishes it.'

'I can't do that, John. I would always see myself as a weakling, unable to provide enough for my own family.'

'I thought you just said that God had spoken to you about your bull-headedness. You can't always rely just upon yourself for everything. Look at your own father. He did his very best for your mother, but no one could have foreseen what eventually happened. You must learn to place your trust in God, not in yourself.'

Colin was tired of arguing. He didn't bother to say any more, instead he closed his eyes. 'I'm sorry, John,' he murmured. 'I've got to get some sleep.'

'Will you think about what I've said?' John pursued that one step further.

'I'll think about it, but you and I see very differently on this issue.'

There was nothing else John could do, so he got up to leave.

'I hope you are soon back on your feet, Col. If you must trust in yourself, you can't afford to be lying about on your back forever.'

CHAPTER 15

❧❀❧

*B*y the time Emily was sent back to her aunt's home, she had begun to accept some of the things that Kate had been trying to make her understand. She had acknowledged that perhaps she had been selfish in what she had wanted from Colin Shore. It had not been easy to admit, but when she had thought about it, she had gradually seen that she had never once thought about what was good for Colin Shore, only what was good for her and, in this instance, what made her feel good. This was really a huge step in her thinking and had brought her to the point that she could look at the possibility of marriage in a wholly different light.

Just as Kate had suggested, she began to read and memorise the verses of scripture from 1 Corinthians 13, where the real attributes of love were outlined. It turned out to be a horrible moment of truth to realise that her racing pulse, and floating, excited feelings had less to do with love than it had to do with herself. After all, as the Bible said, love is patient; love is kind; and further down, it described love as not being self-seeking or easily angered. There were so many things that Emily simply had not considered before.

Gradually, as days turned into weeks, Emily began to let go of the infatuation she had held for so long. If she really loved Colin Shore, then she would be prepared to allow the best for him, and in the end, if the best was someone like Kathleen Miller, then so be it. Emily would now submit her plans to God, and let him work out the finer details.

Surprisingly, Lady Wallace was disappointed with this. She had put her whole reputation on the line defending Colin Shore and taking his side, and in doing so she had grown quite fond of the idea of having him in her home. Despite his obvious lack of wealth, Lady Vera had begun to value his many stable and responsible qualities. So when Emily began to preach at her about wanting only what was best for self, and not considering the needs of others, Lady Vera was somewhat irked. She didn't like to admit that she had wanted to control this young man any more than Emily had liked that same challenge. In times past, the grand lady would most likely have created a storm over such ridiculous ideas, and demanded that Reverend Laslett come and talk some sense into the child. But of late, Lady Wallace found that her own heart had been softened, and instead of starting on a tirade, she quietly retreated and examined the thoughts for any points of truth.

One Saturday afternoon, John and Kate were surprised to receive a visit from Lady Wallace. In practice, most visits between them had occurred the other way around, with the folk from the manse travelling up to the estate.

'I may as well come straight to the point,' Lady Vera spoke up. 'I've been thinking about this business of other Christians in the Valley not coming to church. I know we've disagreed on this issue before, but perhaps I may have been too hasty in my opinions.'

'How do you mean, Lady Vera?' John asked, astounded that such an old argument seemed finally ready to be resolved.

'Take the Shore family, for instance. I quite like that Mrs Shore. She is a courageous woman, and most generous in spirit. It seems a shame that someone like her has not had a place to fellowship all these years.'

'And?' John pushed.

'And that Lilly Miller and her husband. They have been very good to my Emily. They seem decent enough people, despite their circumstances. I don't see any reason why they shouldn't join with the rest of us for worship on a Sunday.'

'I'm glad you see it that way,' John spoke easily. 'I have been of that opinion myself for a number of years.'

'Yes! Yes! Let's not drag up old quarrels now. What I want to know is what you intend to do about it?'

'Well, I can speak to the families that have accepted me as their minister. I will invite them to join us on Sundays, but I cannot guarantee that they will necessarily accept.'

'Why shouldn't they?' Lady Vera was tempted to take offence.

'It's just years of living with social expectations and attitudes often affect the poorer folks as much as it does the rich. I shouldn't think that Mrs Shore or her girls will hold back for long. They love your niece very much, and I know they would welcome the excuse to fellowship together on a Sunday. We might not get the same sort of response from all of the Valley folk, however. Your reputation is rather formidable, you realise.'

'I should hope so. I wouldn't like to think that they hold me of no account at all.'

John and Kate smiled at this comment.

'Time and relationship have a way of breaking down many barriers, Lady Wallace,' Kate offered. 'It's because you know the Shores, and Lilly, that you have softened in your attitude toward them. If you were to get to know other families in the Valley, I dare say that you would come to feel the same about them.'

'And what about that young Shore fellow? What has become of him?' Lady Wallace had wanted to ask after Colin from the first, but had waited until now.

'He was dangerously ill for a time, as you no doubt heard,' John informed. 'I believe he is recovering steadily now.'

'Yes, yes! But what about Emily? Doesn't he have any intention of courting her at all?'

'I was under the impression that Emily was willing to let Mr Shore go,' Kate spoke firmly. 'He is not just a horse to be bought for her use, you know.'

'I never thought he was,' Lady Vera spoke crossly. 'I understand Emily's new resolve. I think it is commendable that she is thinking further than just the passion of the moment. Still, I believe that young Mr Shore would be good for her. I know she still admires him greatly, and was under the impression that he had some feeling for her as well.'

'Unfortunately, feeling is not enough,' John began to explain. 'There are other objections in this case.'

'Like what?' Lady Wallace was indignant that someone so low should find any objections at all, once she had given her approval.

John patiently began to relay Colin's reasoning, and why he felt he could never propose to Emily Wallace.

'That's preposterous!' Lady Wallace snorted. 'That sounds just like some sort of excuse I would make. I've never heard of such pride in all my life!'

Kate could not contain her mirth at the irony of the comment.

'All right!' Lady Wallace replied, very put out. 'I have indulged in an amount of pride myself, over the years. I admit it, and hope I have made some effort at recompense. But this is plain nonsense. In fact, it makes me all the more determined to like the boy. If I'd ever had a son, I'm sure he would have been just as hard-headed and difficult to get on with.'

'Your attitude is charming, Lady Wallace,' John smiled. 'I'm sure Colin would be flattered to think that he is just like you.'

'And so my niece is to live out the rest of her days thwarted in love because he can't accept even a dowry?'

'It would appear so,' John confirmed.

'Well! I see we shall have to think about the problem some more. He has nothing, and will not ask Emily to share poverty with him. She has money, but he will not accept anything he has not worked for with sweat and tears. Is that correct?'

John nodded.

'The only other answer is, if he has wealth of his own, enough to support Emily in a lifestyle she is used to.'

'Yes,' John agreed, 'but that seems to be a most unlikely event to occur.'

'We shall see!' Lady Wallace tilted her chin in a determined slant. 'We shall see!'

Colin sat at home alone on Sunday morning. He was annoyed at his mother and sisters when they had jumped at the chance to attend the Green Valley church. All of these years, they had worshipped together at home. After his father had died, Colin had shared the responsibility of praying and reading the Bible with his mother.

And now, just because Lady Wallace had taken another whim, he was left alone to stew on what had happened. Of course, the invitation to attend the service had been extended to him as well, but he had turned it down immediately.

'Why, Col?' Christine had wailed. 'Why can't we go?'

'Because it's not for us. We don't belong there.'

'I don't agree with you son,' Rose argued. 'We are as much a part of the body of Christ as anyone else on this earth.'

'But we do not belong to that class of people. You know that!'

'Class has nothing to do with faith. Jesus Christ died for all men, and commanded us to love one another. He never said anything about restricting our love to a certain group of people.'

In truth, Colin didn't really mind the idea of mixing with other people from a different station in life. It was more the fact that he could not see Emily any more. He did not want to face all the desire he still had for her, and have to fight it down yet again. And so he hid behind this thin argument, electing to stay at home alone while his mother, sisters and brother went happily to church.

When they arrived home, they were full of excited chatter, obviously having been blessed by the opportunity to gather with other people.

'Of course, I thought Mrs Booth would burst her seams to see us there,' Christine giggled. 'All of these years, she has fancied herself just that one cut above the rest of us.'

'You mustn't start to gossip like that, Christine,' her mother warned. 'This opportunity has come because Lady Wallace has had a change of heart. We don't want to spoil the outcome by becoming spiteful ourselves, do we?'

'Oh, and Col,' June was determined not to miss out on her turn at describing the morning, 'Lady Wallace asked where you were.'

'And what did you tell her?' Colin asked, his unhappy mood showing in his tone.

'We told her that you didn't want to come,' June answered truthfully.

'Yes, and I know someone who was very disappointed to hear it,' Julianne added. She waited, expecting Colin to ask who, but he knew to whom she was referring. He had no wish to talk about Emily Wallace, not when he was spending every last bit of energy to drive her from his thoughts.

That Sunday was followed by many similar Sundays, and each time, Colin refused to join the rest of the family in worship. Even when his friend, Ned Miller, rode over to ask him why he wouldn't go, Colin seemed more resolute than ever.

'Don't tell me you've got all this fanciful nonsense in your head too. Lady Wallace is just playing a game with us. It won't be long and she will be tired of it, and then she won't want to see any of us anymore.'

'I don't know how you can say that,' Ned objected strongly. 'You really should be ashamed of yourself, after all the things she did to defend you in court.'

'It was because of her that I was in court in the first place,' Colin argued.

'I suppose you're going to tell me that you're sorry that you came to Emily Wallace's aid. Is that it? If that man came back again, you'd just ignore her and leave her to his mercy.'

'Shut up, Ned! You don't know what you're talking about.'

'No! You shut up, Col. I admit that I was disappointed with what you did to Kathleen. It was a fairly low thing to do. But when I knew why you did it, I was prepared to forgive you. I know what it's like to be in love, mate. I just don't understand why you're so intent on hurting Emily as well. What has she ever done to you?'

'I don't want to talk about it, Ned!' Colin turned away from him and went about shovelling oats into the pig troughs.

'Is that why you never drop over to our place any more? You don't want to talk about it then, either?'

'Listen! If you're finished with your meddling, would you mind leaving me to get on with some work?'

'Fine!' Ned touched his hat, and mounted his horse. 'When you do want to talk, Col, you know where I live.'

Colin didn't turn to watch his friend ride off. He was angry with himself, and with everyone else who was trying to get him to admit his feelings. That was the real reason he hadn't been to visit with the Millers. He knew that Emily spent a lot of time with Lilly, and he didn't want to risk seeing her.

Just give me some time, he thought. *It won't be too long and I will hardly be able to remember who she even is.*

But if he thought it would go away that easily, he was sorely mistaken. It wasn't too long after Ned's visit that Colin came inside to a very excited sister.

'Guess what, Col,' Christine gushed. 'You are going to be so happy.'

'What? Are you getting married too?'

'It's nearly as good,' Christine hedged. 'One day soon, Julianne will finally marry Pete, and then you will be rid of two of us. That ought to make you happy.'

'Christine,' Rose admonished. 'I don't think you should assume that your leaving home will automatically make your brother happy. I'm sure he has some affection for you in his heart.'

'Mmph! He sure doesn't show any affection for us,' she complained.

'What are you talking about, leaving home?' Colin was at least curious, and perhaps more afraid than he would admit. Though he complained about his sisters often, he'd never actually thought about what it would mean if they left.

'I have a job,' Christine gushed. 'A living away from home job.'

'I didn't know you had been looking,' Colin was flustered. 'I mean, I hope you didn't think I was trying to get rid of you.'

'Oh, no!' Christine was quite sarcastic in her remark. 'Little comments like, "there are too many women in this house", and "I can't wait until you get married" – I would never think you were trying to get rid of us.'

'Christine,' Rose warned again.

'I'm sorry, Christine,' Colin apologised in a genuine tone. 'I didn't realise that I was being so hard to live with.'

'Well, you were. Anyway, now I have a job, and I'm very happy about it.'

'Who will you be working for?' he asked.

'Someone you know very well.'

'Who?' he demanded.

'Lady Wallace, and Miss Emily.'

'What?' His reaction came almost as an explosion. 'What are you going to work for them for?'

'Because there is a position, and I like Emily very much. She is one of my good friends.'

'Some sort of friend. Now you will be her servant!'

'Sort of!' Christine answered cryptically.

'What do you mean sort of?'

'Oh, for goodness sake, Christine!' Julianne broke into the exchange. 'Will you just tell him and let all of us have some peace.'

'Lady Wallace has asked me if I would like to be a companion for them.'

'A companion!'

'You know, like a friend.'

'A paid friend!' Colin sounded astonished.

'She doesn't have to pay me for being a friend,' Christine argued, 'but she will pay for my food and board, and give me an allowance.'

'I don't believe this,' Colin turned to the washstand and began to pour out some water to wash.

'It is a very good opportunity,' Christine defended.

'Sounds great!' Colin answered, between muffled splashes of water on his face. 'You can sit up at the Wallace mansion and drink tea and walk around the garden, and be paid for it into the bargain.'

'But there will be more to do when we go to England.'

This was the shock that she had been keeping all along.

'What did you say?' Colin asked sternly, turning around slowly to face his sister.

'I said that I will be going to England with Emily.'

'No, you will not! You're not going anywhere at all!'

'You can't stop me, Col. I have Mother's permission, and I don't intend to turn down a grand opportunity like this.' Christine had known that her brother would act like this. That was why she had left the part about England until the last.

'The trip to England is just talk at this stage,' Rose tried to reassure her son. 'Even if they eventually went, it wouldn't be for months.'

'I don't care when it is. I don't want her leaving this country.'

The Shore household became very quiet after this exchange. The family ate the evening meal in silence, different ones stewing over different thoughts. Christine was angry with her brother for objecting so readily, without giving the prospect any proper consideration. But she could not have known that it wasn't so much that she had a job, as much as who it was she would be work-ing for. And when he had heard about the plans to go back to England, Colin was all but in a panic. They had just chased Derickson from this country, without the pair of them following him. It was only asking for more trou-ble in his opinion. He'd already made up his mind that he would do everything in his power to keep Christine home, especially if it meant that Emily would stay as well. Obviously they'd all forgotten the threat of Derickson, or they'd never even have discussed such an idea.

Nothing more was said about Christine's position. Rose informed Colin that Christine would be moving to the mansion within the week, and he had nothing left to say about it. When the day came that she finally left, he offered her an affectionate hug, and told her he would miss her.

Christine left, and Colin felt her absence keenly. He never thought he could miss that extra bit of crowding in the house, but he did. And what was worse, he didn't feel as if he could visit her either. So he went about his work, still stubbornly refusing to go to church, and still hesitant to visit with Ned and Lilly.

It seemed like weeks since Colin had seen or heard from Emily Wallace, and each day he tried to pretend to himself that he was thinking of her less and less.

Pete Browning had been around to talk with him about his getting married.

'I don't think it will be as long as we had first thought,' Pete told Colin. 'I just need to get some money together really. Jack is only just sixteen, but Dad seems willing to let me go. I've hated having to wait to get married. I love your sister you know.'

'I've noticed,' Colin answered dryly.

'When I do get the money, it will probably be only just enough to get us over to the colony in South Australia. There is a whole lot of new land being leased by the crown. I reckon I could get some work as a labourer for a year or so, and then we could buy a lease. We probably won't ever come back here, you know.'

Colin did know that, but he hadn't really thought about it up until now. Julianne's promise that one day she would be married had seemed so far off, almost impossible, that Colin hadn't ever wondered what it would really be like to say goodbye to the eldest of his sisters, never to see her again. Not having seen Christine in a number of weeks had made the prospect all the more prominent in his mind, and he wondered how he would ever let Julianne go, and then Samantha and June after. It was just one more emotional turmoil to add to his growing list.

Emily had given up talking about Colin, though she still prayed for him every night. Each time she brought him to the Lord in prayer, she asked that God would bring the very best thing for him into his life. She also asked that God would either take away the feelings she had for him, or that he would fulfil them. Emily Wallace had come a long way since her talk with Kate Laslett. She had begun to listen carefully to the minister's wife, and had begun to follow her advice. Instead of looking to a man to bring the relief from hurt she suffered, she started to look to God. At first she was amazed to find that He really did answer those sorts of prayers. Day by day, she became stronger and more confident. There were occasional lapses into fear and doubt, but time spent talking with Kate, and praying together usually brought Emily back to stable ground.

And then, of course, Christine had come to live with them. It didn't take long for the two girls to become almost as close as sisters. Together they talked and planned outings, and even talked about England and what it held for Emily.

Emily had no real desire to return to the land of her birth, now that her father was gone and with Derickson there and threatening. But there were legal and financial matters that needed her attention. Her aunt had discussed it all with her, and had made contact with James Melville, her sister Muriel's son, to see if he would be willing to act on Emily's behalf. But when Emily talked about it with Christine, it was obvious that, her financial affairs notwithstanding, she was quite reluctant to go, even temporarily. It was Emily who suggested that they pray together about this and many other things. As Emily's close friend and confidant, Christine grew in her own confidence, and Emily, in turn, became more familiar with the ways of the Australian countrywoman.

The girls sometimes talked about what might have been.

'I would really have liked to have had you as a sister-in-law,' Christine confessed.

'And I you. I think your family is wonderful.' Emily returned the compliment.

'My brother is as stubborn as a mule! You know that, don't you?'

'I don't blame him, in one way,' Emily defended Colin. 'He has to have some self-respect. I can't expect him to just accept all of my ways. I am a spoiled little rich girl, after all.'

'You've changed though, Emily,' Christine observed. 'You were a little bit demanding before, but lately, you seem to be much more sensitive to other people.'

'Thanks, Christine. That's a compliment.'

Emily was thankful for Christine's company and friendship. She had grown to love her aunt almost as the mother she hardly remembered, but Christine was a breath of fresh air by comparison; someone her own age, who had similar interests and hopes. It became slightly easier as week by week passed. Emily had got over hoping that perhaps today she would see Colin again. She still prayed for him, but only ever talked of him when Christine brought up the subject.

And so Emily certainly didn't expect the encounter that came: nor had she any idea that it would be so devastating to her.

Kate had asked if Emily and Christine would like to visit for the day. She had shared with the younger girls her good news of expecting another child, and had to confess that she wished they would play with her girls. Kate had been suffering with morning sickness, and her two daughters were past the stage where she could expect them to take an afternoon nap.

'Please,' she begged. 'If you could just amuse them for a few hours, I would be forever grateful. Take them for a walk; read them a story; teach them to bake biscuits. I don't care at the moment. I just feel too sick.'

Though neither Christine nor Emily had any idea of the misery that morning sickness could bring, they could see that the minister's wife needed help, and so they happily agreed to take care of Elizabeth and Annie. Emily suggested that they do the home activities first, and then take the girls out for a long walk.

'Perhaps we will wear the little darlings out, and they will be ready for a nap.'

After having allowed them to mix up a batch of biscuits, getting flour and sugar all over the kitchen floor,

Emily sat and read them two stories from their storybook, while Christine graciously offered to clean up. Then the two young women took a child each by the hand, and they set off into the warm afternoon, determined not to return until the little girls complained of being tired.

The idea worked, and Christine smiled, satisfied, as they tucked Kate's tired out daughters in to their beds. It was then that they became aware that the reverend had a visitor. Not wanting to intrude, they consulted in whispered tones, and decided to sit quietly in the kitchen until the visitor had left. They didn't know that what they were about to hear accidentally would be the final straw of disappointment for Emily's hopes.

'I can't believe she would stoop to this,' Colin's angry tone penetrated through into the kitchen. Christine recognised his voice immediately, and looked to her companion for confirmation. She could see that Emily had also guessed who it was.

'The high and mighty Miss Wallace has finally got her own way.'

'What are you talking about, Col?' John didn't know that Emily was in the house, or he would have attempted to quieten his friend down.

'Look at this, would you,' Colin hit a sheaf of papers with the back of his hand. 'The ultimate manipulation.'

'What is it?' John was disturbed at Colin's accusations.

'Do you know what she did?'

'Who?'

'Emily Wallace!' Colin was frustrated that John hadn't understood from the first.

'What has Emily done that has made you so angry?'

'She has tricked her aunt into this – this sham!' He threw the papers down on the table in disgust.

'What's in the papers?' John asked, trying to make sense of the situation.

'She had that fancy lawyer from Melbourne come out to my farm to deliver them to me. He wanted me to sign, but I wouldn't!'

'What are the papers, Col?' John's voice rose in authority.

'It's her will.'

'Whose will?'

'Lady Wallace's. Emily has talked her into signing over the entire Wallace estate to me. I am now named as the sole heir of Lady Vera Wallace.'

'You are joking, Colin, aren't you?' John was not sure.

'No! I'm not joking. Just you look at all of this fancy paperwork.' Colin picked up the pile again, and began to point out certain paragraphs that were relevant to him.

'See,' he announced. 'Not only that, but she has signed over her power of attorney to me, now. As the lawyer said to me, I am now wholly responsible for the success or failure of Lady Wallace's interests.'

'And what did you say?'

'What could I say? I wouldn't sign the papers. I told him I never would. I cannot believe that she would stoop to such a low trick.'

'You think that Emily has put her aunt up to this?'

'Of course! I mean, I know I have been smitten by the girl, but I meant what I said about us. I will be the man in my own home. I won't have it any other way. If I ever took hold of Emily's money, or Lady Wallace's, I would never be able to respect myself again.'

'And so you think that Emily has designed this so that you can have money of your own.'

'Yes! But she's gone too far this time. I don't plan to inherit somebody else's fortune. I plan to make my own way.'

'Actually, Col, the heir doesn't have any say about it. It is the will of the benefactor.'

'Yes, well this particular heir has no intention of taking any such responsibility. I have my own land, and my own family to support. I don't need her money, or anyone else's.'

'Have you spoken to Lady Wallace about this?' John asked.

'No!'

'Don't you think you should?'

'Why?'

'Because she obviously has some strong feelings about what she wants for her future, and she apparently believes that you should be a part of it.'

Emily had listened to only about half of this exchange. She had heard all of the accusations against her, and though Christine tried to stop her, she made for the back door, and ran out into the afternoon air. Christine, of course, ran out after her.

'I don't know what he's talking about,' Emily sobbed. 'I don't know what Aunt Vera has done, but I didn't have anything to do with it. Why is he so angry with me?'

'There, there. Stop it, Emily. Colin is a bumble-headed fool sometimes. Don't pay any attention to his raving.'

'But he said that I had done the ultimate in trying to manipulate him. He said that I had tricked my aunt.'

'We both know that isn't true.'

'But Aunt Vera must have left him something in her will, and he won't take it.'

'If he hasn't got the good sense to see a blessing when it comes along then that's his own silly fault, Emily.'

'But you know that means that even when he has the opportunity, he doesn't want me. He doesn't love me. Perhaps he never really did.'

'I don't know, Emily.' Christine had thought her brother did love Emily, but he had been acting so strangely of late that she had begun to wonder.

'I want to go home,' Emily cried.

'All right. You just wait a moment, and I will tell Kate that we are leaving.'

'No! You don't understand. I want to go back home, to England.'

'England!' Christine cried. 'We haven't heard from James Melville yet. I would feel much happier if we knew that Mr Melville was going to meet us and take care of all the details. I don't know if it's sensible to be going, otherwise! Remember Lord Derickson and all.'

'They will take me,' Emily said. 'Aunt Vera has had a letter from her sister this morning.'

'Emily!' Christine was scared by her friend's distress. 'Not yet. Just give it some time. Perhaps you'll feel differently in a few days.'

'No! I can't stay here any more. I love you, and I love my aunt, but I can't stay here when he doesn't want me. He thinks I have tried to trap him. I haven't. Not like that, have I?'

'Come on, Emily. You're distraught now. Let's just go back to your aunt's and have a cup of tea.'

Christine managed to guide Emily to the waiting horses, and the pair finally found their way back to the Wallace estate, but Emily was in such a state of misery, that Christine didn't know if she would ever be able to talk her out of it.

CHAPTER 16

olin had never been more angry in his life. He had seen just how powerful the rich could be, in fact he had scars on his body to show what sort of influence they wielded; scars that had been inflicted at the whim of Derickson, just because he had wanted revenge. And now Emily was showing her true colours.

Colin cursed himself again at having become so emotionally attached to the young woman. But in a way, he was glad that he had found out. Now he could let go of her in his mind, thankful that he had not yielded to her supposed power to control.

Still, he knew that something had to be done about the matter of the will. He didn't know to what extent Lady Wallace had lost authority over her own affairs, and he was decent enough to at least inquire after her welfare.

'I hope it's not too late to reverse this mess your niece has put you in,' Colin spoke firmly. 'You cannot know how sorry I am that you have been put in this difficult position.'

'What mess?' Lady Vera seemed confused.

'This business of the will.'

'What has my niece done to my will?'

'I suspected that you had nothing to do with it,' Colin confessed. 'I wish I weren't the one who had to inform you.'

'Inform me of what, young man?' Lady Wallace sounded stern.

'It would seem that Miss Emily has manipulated the situation, I don't know how she's done it, but I have been informed that I am your sole heir.'

'Oh! Thank goodness!' Lady Vera breathed her relief. 'For a moment there, I thought you were going to tell me that she had destroyed the will or something.'

'Don't you understand?' Colin looked at her with some form of sympathy. 'This will says that I am to inherit your entire estate, and that I am now in charge of it, even before you die.'

'That is the paper I signed,' Lady Vera acknowledged.

'What has Miss Emily done to force you to do such a stupid thing?'

'Emily? I doubt she even knows about it!' Lady Vera stared knowingly at her visitor. 'I see that you suspect my niece of foul play.'

Colin was stuck for an answer.

'Making you my heir was my idea, and mine alone.'

'But why?' Colin was astounded.

'Several reasons,' she offered. 'Firstly, I value your honesty, responsibility and determination to succeed. I have also noticed a good deal of stubborn pride, a quality that I have made good use of myself, over the years. I never had a son, Mr Shore, but if I had ever been so blessed, I would have wanted someone very like you.'

'But that is no reason to hand over your entire life's work to someone you hardly know,' Colin argued. 'It seems to me as if perhaps it is you who is manipulating the situation. Does this have anything to do with your niece?'

'You won't marry her if you cannot support her, isn't that so?' Lady Vera asked directly.

'I'm not about to . . . to . . . take all of this,' he waved his hand to indicate the expanse of the room, 'just so I can marry your niece. I'm not one of your lazy, money-grabbing lords who'll do anything to get out of working for their keep.'

'That is another reason why I named you, and not one of them,' Lady Wallace stated. 'I believe you will work this land and make it prosper even more than I have been able to do. I don't need some fat, pompous gentleman here, barking orders thoughtlessly, not knowing one end of a cow from the other. You know your business, and you will make the best of mine.'

'I won't take it!' Colin sounded resolute.

'Then the land will gradually deteriorate until it fails,' Vera said equally as stubbornly, 'and all of my employees will be without support or income.'

'You tell me this so that I will marry your niece. That's blackmail!'

'Whether you marry Emily or not, the will remains as it is written. This land is yours to work or to neglect. I have wiped my hands of all responsibility.'

Colin stared at her, open-mouthed, amazed at the strength of resolve this woman displayed.

'I can't accept it!' he finally said emphatically.

'I didn't really think you would. You are a proud young man, perhaps even more proud than I have been in the past. Let me give you a word of advice, Mr Shore, and I believe Reverend Laslett would be proud of me in this.

'The Lord God has given a rich inheritance of eternal life and earthly blessing, paid for by the death of his Son, Jesus Christ. He has made it abundantly clear that all people are equal in their right to claim this inheritance, and yet multitudes of men and women refuse to take a hold of his promises, just as you are doing here; and why? Pride; stubbornness; rebellion. It seems that any excuse will do. So what does God do with his will? Does he change it, just because his people refuse to take a hold of it?'

She paused, waiting for Colin to respond, but he had no words to answer.

'God's will doesn't change, Mr Shore. And I have to say, neither will mine. If Emily does go back to England, and we never see her again, you will still be the heir to my fortune.'

Colin left Lady Wallace, stunned and amazed. He had heard what she had said, and he had understood what she meant, but he could not understand why she was doing it. She was even prepared to allow her niece to return to England, and still let go of her authority to him. It didn't make any sense, and he wondered if it might not have been some sort of elaborate joke.

But the more he thought about it, and the more he read through the papers outlining the legality of the arrangements, the more he began to believe that what she had said was true.

And yet, the struggle with his pride was enormous. He didn't go to discuss the issue with John any more. He still wouldn't go to church, or to visit his friends. All his self-respect would allow him to do was to throw himself into his own farm responsibilities.

Though Rose was aware that something had arisen with regard to Lady Wallace, she did not know the exact nature of the situation; neither did she ask. She waited patiently for her son to reveal his worries to her. But Colin had almost succeeded in pushing the will and its responsibilities from his mind. Rose saw Emily and Christine at church and, once again, she could see that something was amiss. Emily was miserable, perhaps even depressed. Christine, who would have shared the circumstances with her mother, did not feel it was her right to talk about all that had gone on. And so Rose remained ignorant to the finer details, wishing that she could speak encouragement, but unable to offer any such words to either Emily or Colin.

Several weeks after the incident at the manse, Colin met Ned, and the two of them rounded up stock to take to the market in Brinsford. At first, Colin was sullen and spoke only of the quality of animal, or to exchange plans about the best way to load their stock onto the wagon.

The pair set out from Green Valley, expecting to take at least two days to make it to Brinsford and back, providing nothing happened to delay them. At first, Ned was cautious about touching on delicate subjects. He had already faced Colin's wrath when they had last spoken, and he didn't feel equal to another loud confrontation.

'Lilly has recovered really quickly since the birth of Edward,' Ned said by way of conversation. 'Having three little ones sure is a handful. I can just imagine what the noise level will be like when we have more children.'

'How many children do you think you will be able to fit in that small place?' Colin asked, an obvious bitterness colouring his tone.

'If God blesses my home with children, then He will make sure I can look after them.' Ned seemed firm in his reply.

'That sounds like a simple sort of answer. Don't you ever wonder if God might think it's wiser for us not to have children in the first place?'

'Children are the fruit of marriage, my friend. I love my wife, and together we will accept the responsibility of our union.'

'But what about when you don't have enough to feed them all, or enough to clothe them properly? What about if you have a bad year, and there just isn't enough to go around?'

'I'm not going to worry about bad things that might happen, not when I can thank God for the good things that are here now.'

'I can't see that more children are a blessing when I'm scratching around trying to provide for what I've already got.'

'You will change your tune when your first child is born,' Ned thumped him on the arm playfully. 'There is no greater miracle in my book.'

'I don't plan to marry,' Colin stated as if it meant nothing at all. 'If I don't have a wife, then I won't need to worry about more mouths to feed.'

'Col! That is the most ridiculous thing I've heard you say yet!'

'Why? Just because you got yourself married isn't any reason that all of us must follow along.'

'What about love?' Ned asked, frustrated with his partner.

'Love? What about it?'

'I know you were in love, Col. Don't try to deny it. Surely you don't want to live your whole life without fully experiencing what you felt?'

'I can't afford to fall in love. I simply can't afford it!'

'Ah, that's nonsense. Love doesn't cost you anything.'

'Doesn't it?'

'Well, other than giving of yourself, patience and gentleness; things like that.'

'And what about supporting a lifestyle?'

'Emily Wallace has money. We've been through this before, I think.'

'And I told you I'm not going to take her money.'

'What about your money. The Wallace estate.'

'How did you hear about that?' Colin turned an angry eye on his friend.

'You forget. Lilly has become quite close to Emily. Several weeks back, Emily suddenly stopped coming to visit, so Lilly took the children up to the mansion to see if she was ill. Emily told Lilly what her aunt had done, and the rotten things you had said about her.'

'What do you mean?' Suddenly, Colin was curious and afraid all at once.

'The way I heard it, you accused Emily of scheming against her aunt, and tricking her into this will thing. Lilly told me that she had never seen Emily so upset and depressed in all the time she's known her.' Ned watched for Colin's response, and when there was only a stunned silence, he went on. 'I suppose you're going to tell me that you never accused Emily of anything of the kind.'

'I . . . well, I didn't . . . I don't know how she could have heard me say those things,' Colin stuttered.

'Emily and Christine were at the manse the day you shouted out your anger with John. They heard everything you said.'

'Oh no!' Colin closed his eyes against the realisation of what he'd done. 'Does she know that I know the truth now?'

'I haven't heard that much. All I know is that Emily is seriously talking about going back to England.'

'England?'

'You know! The land where she came from. She has a brother there, and a fortune to inherit.'

'And Lord Richard Derickson! I won't let her go!'

'Fine words from a man who has no right to say them!'

Colin was seriously taken aback. Ned was right. He was nothing to Emily Wallace and had no say in what she did or didn't do.

'You don't know what her brother will force her to do,' Colin argued. 'He doesn't care what sort of man Derickson is.'

'And you do?' Ned pushed.

'You know I do,' Colin answered angrily.

'So what are you going to do about it?'

'What can I do?'

'If she were your wife, then you could look out for her interests. Take care of her, love her and help her sort out her affairs with her brother.'

'But how can I marry her. I can't support her, you know that!'

'Can't you? What about the Wallace estate. Isn't that yours to do with as you will?'

'Are you seriously saying I should accept Lady Wallace's will?'

'I'm saying that the land is yours whether you accept it or not. Why on earth can't you just make it work for you, and help the woman you love at the same time? It's really not that difficult, Col.'

'But what about my own land?' Colin's former resolve was weakening.

'Why don't you let Pete and Julianne have your father's land? Give it to them as a wedding present.'

'I guess that would mean they could get married sooner.' Colin was beginning to warm to the idea. 'And Pete never really wanted to leave Green Valley.'

'Exactly!' Ned seemed happy that he had finally gotten through. 'Imagine how your sisters will just love living in such a grand house.'

'You mean, we would all shift in with Lady Wallace? I don't know about that.'

'What's to know? How many bedrooms has that mansion got anyway?'

'Well, I'm not really sure, but I suppose there would have to be about ten or so. But it's Lady Wallace's house really.'

'I'm not suggesting you throw her out, Col. Surely the house is big enough for you all to live in without getting in each other's way.'

'I don't know if that's what Lady Wallace really had in mind. I mean, without Julianne, there are still six of us, and none of us are what you would call refined.'

'Don't you think you should at least discuss the idea with her first, before dismissing it altogether?' Ned seemed to have gained the upper hand in the argument and was now pressing for a conclusion. 'You know, I have the impression that Lady Wallace doesn't really want her niece to go back to England. I'd think she'd do just about anything to see her stay here.'

'Like will her estate to a no-account farmer!' Colin expressed his suspicions again.

'I think she has proved that there were other motives as well for making that decision. It seems that she has really taken to you.'

Colin began to think about all the things that he'd discussed with Ned. They talked some more, but it always seemed to lead to the same conclusion. Colin began to believe that he could actually accept the estate, and that there was perhaps a chance that he could ask Emily Wallace to marry him; of course that was if she was prepared to forgive him for his dreadful outburst at the manse.

Even though the stock didn't fetch quite the price Colin had hoped for, nothing seemed as desperate as it had before. The more he considered the idea, the more he began to understand just what sort of responsibility being the manager, soon to be owner, of the Wallace estate meant. There were times when his brain refused to comprehend just how much land and stock the grand lady was offering him. Still, by the time Ned had dropped him back to his home, two and a half days later, Colin was sure of what he was going to do next.

'Did you get the money you wanted for those sheep?' Rose asked, when they sat down to dinner.

'Not quite, but it doesn't matter any more.'

'Doesn't matter?' Rose questioned, surprised at his relaxed tone. 'Normally you'd have come in demanding that we cut back on our food until we had better times. Why doesn't it matter this time?'

'It's a long story, Mum.' Colin realised that he hadn't ever mentioned the matter of the will to his mother, and didn't feel like going into it now.

'What's a long story?' She wasn't quite so easily satisfied.

'I'll tell you about it, soon, but I have a visit to make first.'

'Colin! What is going on? This is very unusual behaviour for you.'

'Is it?' He seemed genuinely amazed.

'Yes, it is.'

'I'm sorry. Do you think that Lady Wallace would object to visitors this time of the evening?' Colin did not have his thoughts on his mother's questions, and completely changed the subject.

'Colin! You haven't been out visiting anyone at all in weeks, and now you want to travel in the twilight to call on the patron lady of Green Valley?'

'Yes! Well, I have some things I need to sort out with her,' he went on, 'and I thought I might catch up with Christine.'

'Christine, or Emily?' Now Rose was beginning to understand his mental dithering.

'It would be nice to see Miss Emily again,' Colin admitted that much.

'I'm sure it would be, after all this time, except that you're too late.'

'Do you think so? Do you think I should wait until tomorrow?'

'No!' Rose objected. 'You don't understand. I mean you won't be able to catch up with either of them for a long time, maybe forever. They left for Melbourne two days ago, and planned to catch the first ship to England from there.'

CHAPTER 17

Colin had not felt such panic in all his life; not even when he was being dragged behind the trooper's horse and in danger of his life. Shouting unreasonable accusations at his mother had not changed the facts, and he was now faced with a horrible prospect; something he had tried to pretend would not matter; the idea of losing Emily Wallace.

'Why didn't you stop them?' Colin asked his mother again, in a raised voice. 'You shouldn't have let them go.'

'I told you, son,' Rose began again, 'Christine was given this grand opportunity, and I wasn't about to deny her the chance to have such a great experience.'

'What about Derickson? Has everyone taken leave of their senses? Has no one thought about what he could do?'

'Quite certainly!' Rose said with a firm tone. 'Lady Wallace would never have allowed them to go if her nephew hadn't agreed to meet them and act as guardian and protector. Neither would I.'

'But Derickson's there, and so will they be,' Colin objected.

'Lady Wallace has had legal documentation from the magistrate in Brinsford outlining Derickson's behaviour and sentence. James Melville will make sure the girls are well protected.'

'Well, you should have made them wait for me to come back.'

'As far as I knew, you wanted nothing to do with Emily Wallace. Christine told me that you had been quite cruel to the girl. How was I to know what was going on in your mind?'

'But you could have made Christine wait, at least.'

'I did suggest it, but she was quite adamant that they start their journey straight away as they'd arranged to travel with a couple Reverend Laslett knows from Melbourne. I thought perhaps you might have seen them in Brinsford. Hodges drove them to meet the train.'

'And who went with them to Melbourne? Who's going to look after them on their way to England?'

'Colin, I do wish you would be reasonable. Even if I had wanted to, I could not have stopped them from leaving. Hearing what has gone on between you recently, I am almost of the opinion that Emily is running away from you. If that is the case, it's hardly likely that she's going to stay and wait for you to say goodbye. Were you cruel to the girl, Col?'

'I didn't know she was listening.' Colin excused himself.

'Would it have made any difference if you did? Weren't you still angry at her for something you believed she'd done?'

Colin thought about it for a while, and had to admit that he might very well have flown at her in person had he known she was there.

'I can't do anything about that now,' his thoughts raced on. 'I'll have to go after them.' Having uttered these words, Colin grabbed his coat off the wall peg, and began to pull on his boots again.

'You can't go out in the dark,' Rose objected.

'I can't wait here all night,' Colin countered. 'I have to get to them before they board a ship. If I don't . . . . ' He let his words trail away. In fact, he didn't really want to think about what he would do if he got to Melbourne and found that the girls had already left for England. At the very least, it would take up to a year to contact them again, unless he took the next ship after them. The whole possibility was too hard to think about and Colin stood up ready to leave.

'If I can't talk you into waiting until morning, could I at least make you take some extra clothing and some food?'

'I don't have time,' Colin replied without thought.

'I'll only take two minutes. Surely you can spare that much time.'

'Hurry up, then.' Colin was agitated, terse and past being civil with his mother. If Rose had not fully understood his worry, she could easily have been angered by his behaviour.

Having accepted the small flour bag of provisions, and taken the drawstring bag with some extra clothes in it, Colin left the small house and set out into the night. His horse was not anxious to be out of its stall and away from its food, but Colin was determined to get underway at once.

Riding in the dim starlight meant much slower travel than if he'd been able to spur the horse into a full gallop, safe only in broad daylight, and consequently, the journey that would have taken a little over two hours normally, took almost double that time. Colin approached the town of Brinsford close to midnight. There were only one or two lights that still glowed from house windows, at that time of the night.

Colin was too full of his own distress to take any thought for the families that were still awake, possibly dealing with some night-time dilemma. Now he was faced with a dark and lifeless railway station. He had not considered that there would not be a train waiting for him to simply jump aboard. Of course, the other time he had gone to Melbourne, the time when he had first met Emily, John had known when the train was scheduled for departure, and so naturally there was a train waiting to take them immediately away.

Now, Colin was faced with the prospect of having to sleep for the rest of the night hours, and possibly having to wait for any number of hours in the morning. Even then, he had to admit that he didn't know the frequency of the trains through Brinsford, and then the possibility that he might even have to wait for days hit him with full force.

I will ride all the way to Melbourne, he finally decided, before drifting into a fitful slumber about two in the morning.

Emily was torn by warring emotions. On the one hand, she didn't want to even consider leaving this land she had grown to love. Other than some matters pertaining to her mother's estate, there was nothing in England for her now. Really all Emily could really count on in that distant place was that her brother would not take any action on her behalf. But she had chased these thoughts from her mind. She couldn't stay here in Australia any more. There was no possible way that she could ever face Green Valley again; not with the likelihood of seeing Colin Shore again.

How that man had hurt her. She had lost her heart to him months ago, she knew that. And she also knew that she had not behaved in a proper manner, really. Of course, if she had been with the young ladies of English society, they would not have frowned at her motives. In fact, she probably would have been one of many vying for his attention.

But here in rural Australia, the ideas were different. Perhaps, in a way, they were even more proper than the endless etiquette of her own culture. Kate Laslett probably would have called it being more considerate and loving for other people. And really, that was the bottom line. She had not been considerate or loving in her motives. But she had acknowledged that, and had repented. She had even come to the point where she was willing to let Colin go, to marry Kathleen Miller. But for him to turn around and accuse her of manipulating her aunt into giving up her property; for him to believe that she would even try to trick her aunt, that was a hard thing for her to bear. And so her resolve to escape had brought her this far.

Christine, of course, had made minor objections to their leaving, but on the whole, she was full of the excitement of a new adventure.

'Are you nervous, Emily?' Christine asked, her own jittery state quite obvious. 'To think that we will step on to that ship today, and tomorrow we will be far away from home. Oh! I wonder if we're doing the right thing.'

Emily could not have answered her companion if she had tried. She didn't want to leave; she was scared of leaving, even with the elderly couple along who had agreed to act as chaperones for the trip. But there was no other choice in her mind. She could not face the pain of seeing Colin Shore again.

In stark contrast to Christine's wide-eyed excitement, Emily accepted the tickets from the shipping clerk with a dull expression of thanks.

'Your trunks will be taken on board to your cabin, Miss,' he explained. 'Perhaps you have family you want to say goodbye to? Passengers won't need to go aboard for another hour, if you have other things to attend to.'

Emily gave a wan smile of thanks, but she had no intention of waiting on shore. She wanted to find her cabin and lie down; she wanted to chase away the pain in her heart.

'I think we should just go aboard.' Emily turned and spoke to their companions and they agreed to meet them aboard, after bidding farewell to their own family.

'Well, it's fine with me!' Christine couldn't wait to begin exploring the massive transport.

'Come on, then.' Emily began to walk wearily out of the waiting room, busily chasing away memories of her first experience in this very room. Once again, he was there to taunt her thoughts. She had been so embarrassed by the way she had thrown herself at him, kissing him boldly, having mistaken him for a relative. Oh, if only she could forget all the times she had been close to him. If only she could erase the memory of ever having met him.

'Colin! What on earth are you doing here?' Emily looked up at the sound of Christine's voice. Surely she hadn't heard right. But to her horror, there he was, standing not just as a memory, but larger than life.

'You can't go,' Colin blurted out his one and only thought. 'I won't let you go.'

'You can't stop me,' Christine objected. 'Mum has given me her permission. It is a wonderful opportunity and . . . . '

'Not you,' he spoke thoughtlessly, 'Emily.'

'You're mad, brother dear,' Christine spoke on her friend's behalf. 'Do you honestly think you have any right at all to be making such a statement?'

'Christine, do you mind? Could you give us a moment alone?' Colin spoke to his sister, annoyed.

'I don't think . . . it's not proper,' she replied.

'Hang what's proper,' Colin exploded at her. 'I want to talk to Emily alone.'

'Is that all right with you?' Christine sought Emily's approval.

'Just a few moments, Christine,' Emily confirmed. 'This won't take long.'

Christine graciously moved across to the other side of the room, reassured their chaperones and then turned her back so as not to observe the exchange between her friend and brother.

'I'm sorry, Emily,' Colin began, breathlessly. 'I know you heard me say some stupid things, but now I know that they're not true.'

'Only now?' Emily relived the agony of the hurt. 'You didn't believe it though, until it was proved to you.'

'Well, I thought . . . . '

'Exactly. You thought I was a cheat and a liar.'

'I never said that.'

'No! But you implied it.'

'I was wrong.'

'You were indeed! Anyway, I can see that the whole situation displeases you, so I am removing myself.'

'But I don't want you to go.'

'Why? So you can have the pleasure of knowing I'm sitting about frustrated and miserable, just close enough for you to know that you have this effect on me?'

'I don't want you to be miserable. I don't want to be miserable either.'

'Then let me go, and we can both forget each other.'

'I can't forget you. You're in my every thought. It's as if you belong to me. I need you, Emily.' Colin's words were full of longing.

'What about your pride and principles?' Emily fought to maintain her indignation. 'I thought I was too good for you.'

'You are too good for me.' Colin readily agreed, reaching out to gently take hold of her forearms. 'But you must understand; I can't live without you. I wouldn't blame you for turning me down, but I want you to be my wife.'

Emily wanted to shout at him more, but she had come to the end of her anger. She heard his proposal and, despite the lingering desire to thump her fists on his chest, she couldn't hold out any more. But neither could she respond. It was too sudden a change of emotions for her to automatically become soft and yielding. And so the much despised tears welled up and eventually spilled over their bounds, causing Emily to reach up and quickly wipe them away.

'Please don't cry, Emily.' Colin felt weakened by her expression. 'I know I'm a cad and I don't even deserve the time of day; and I know that I can't even give you everything you're used to. There is not one logical reason why you should accept me at all. Not one. But the truth is, Emily, I love you and I'm lost without you.'

'I'm lost without you, too.' Emily forced these words out, over the sobs that refused to remain at bay. 'I don't care if you haven't got a thing in the world. I never have cared. Ever since I fell in love with you, all I have wanted is to marry you.'

***

Christine knew what the argument in the corner meant. She knew how it would end even before she saw her brother hold Emily close. What it meant to her was the end of the adventure of a lifetime. Somehow, she had known that her obnoxious brother would find a way to spoil this for her too.

'Is the young lady all right?' The clerk's voice broke into Christine's irritated thoughts. 'Is that rough-looking fellow hurting her?'

Christine gave an amused smile. With all of the shouting that had passed back and forth between the pair, she couldn't blame the official for being concerned for Emily's welfare. And Colin was dressed in his normal working clothes, so he looked rather like a bushranger.

'It's all right,' Christine reassured the man. 'That rough looking fellow is my brother, and unless I'm mistaken, he is currently proposing to the young lady.'

EPILOGUE

The one-horse buggy containing two people looked quite out of place as it drew up outside the old Shore place. Whereas the couple were elegantly dressed, and their vehicle was obviously luxurious and quite new, the run down farmhouse gave off a weariness associated with lack of care. It seemed that the pair should simply pass by, as they and the house just didn't match. But instead of driving past, the gentleman driving guided his horse into the yard and got down from his seat, as if he had just come home. Tying the reins of the harness to a hitching post, he then went around to the other side of the buggy and carefully assisted his female companion to the ground, then together they began to unload a number of things that had been stowed under the seat and tied on behind. To a casual observer, the scene would have looked completely wrong; an obvious contradiction in roles. Such a gracious-looking pair could not possibly be taking up residence in such a ramshackle dwelling.

But Mr and Mrs Colin Shore were not moving their belongings in to his father's home. That was not the object of their visit at all.

'Do you know, I always imagined that one day I would bring my bride to this house,' Colin spoke in a pensive tone. 'This is the place I thought I would make a home for my family.'

'And in your dreams, were you happy with your family?' Emily couldn't help asking.

'The happiness I dreamed of has sort of paled when I compare it with what I have.'

Colin opened the door of his former home, and held it open for his wife to pass through.

'Oh, Col,' Emily sighed. 'This place looks so sad without your mother and sisters busy in the kitchen and Harry playing in the corner.'

'Believe me, Harry is much happier playing in his own room, and as for my sisters, don't let me start on them.'

'But I feel so awful having them working in the kitchen at the big house.'

'You'd best let them work, Emily. Mother would die of boredom if we didn't allow her a free reign in the domestic running of the house.'

'But I'm no help to her at all. I've tried to learn all her skills, but she has such a way about her.'

'You are you, Emily. I know she appreciates your company, but I don't think she would ever try to make you into an ordinary farmer's wife.'

'But I want to be an ordinary farmer's wife. I love who you are, and I want to be part of it.'

Colin grinned and took her in an embrace, kissing her forehead as a gesture of his affection. 'Come along, Em. We have work to do here before it gets too late.'

'I'm so glad that Julianne and Pete are going to stay on in Green Valley,' Emily spoke as she began to sweep the floor. 'I hope they'll be happy here in your old home.'

'They're ecstatic.' Colin was confident. 'And I know they were thrilled to be given that honeymoon trip by your aunt. They never expected ever to travel just for the pleasure of it, and to have such grand accommodation arranged for them.'

'I wish we could have given them more,' Emily sighed again.

'There's going to be fuss enough when they return and see the presents you've already bought them. Don't forget just how proud we poor folk can be.'

'Please! Don't remind me of it.'

The young husband and wife worked for the better part of two hours, cleaning out the dust and cobwebs, setting out some brand new china on the new linen tablecloth, and finally, Emily called Colin to help her make up the old double bed.

'I do wish you had let Aunt Vera send out a new bedstead for them,' Emily expressed her thoughts.

'Emily, please. I will have a war on my hands as it is talking them into accepting the china and this fancy piece of work.' Colin was referring to a magnificent satin bedspread with delicate embroidery, overlaid by finely crocheted lace.

'It's beautiful, isn't it?' Emily admired the fine handiwork.

'That may be, but my sister isn't going to let poor old Pete come any where near this bedroom so long as this is on the bed.'

'Why?' Emily's look was puzzlement and offence together.

'Perhaps you have forgotten what real farmers look like when they've come inside after a day's work.'

'Oh dear! Yes, I see what you mean.' Emily smiled as she imagined Julianne's indignation at dust and dirt being dragged anywhere near. 'I wouldn't let you come near it either, if you weren't perfectly clean.'

'Then I'd throw it away,' Colin declared boldly, 'or perhaps we could leave this room just for the looks of it, and you could sleep out in my old bed with me.' He attacked her playfully, and lifted her off the ground, as if to carry out the threat.

But Emily didn't have any inclination to fight him. 'Pete and Julianne are not due back until tomorrow,' she spoke in a low voice. 'Perhaps we could stay in this house just for one night, just as you always dreamed you would.'

'Aren't you afraid that they'll send out a search party looking for us, if we don't return for dinner?'

'They know I'm with you, and we are married now, good sir. Or had you forgotten?'

'I haven't forgotten.' Colin's voice had become husky with emotion. 'Let's just pretend, for one night, that you and I are just as poor as I used to be and that this is the home that I have provided for you. Do you think you could be happy?'

'You are a good man, Colin Shore, and a good husband. Wealthy or not, I love you the way you are.'

'Then, my good lady, this is all the mansion that I really have to offer. How do you like it?'

'I like it very much.' Emily smiled up into his face. 'Except one thing.'

'There's no room for a staircase,' Colin teased.

'No! I don't want a staircase.'

'What is it that you need then?'

'I just need to know exactly where you want to put the cradle.'

'Cradle?' Colin showed his confusion.

'You know, to be ready for when the baby arrives.'

'Baby? We are still pretending, aren't we?'

'Not this time, Col.'

'You're trying to tell me that we are going to have a baby?'

'I know you haven't been very keen on the idea,' Emily was a little nervous. 'Lilly and Ned told me the sorts of things you used to say about extra mouths to feed, but

I'm afraid it's true. God is going to send you an extra mouth to feed. Are you too upset?'

'Upset! I'm shocked!'

'I'm sorry, Col. I had hoped you'd have been perhaps a little bit happy.'

'No! No, Emily. I am happy, at least I will be when I've figured out just how this happened.'

'You're the farmer, Colin. I'd have thought you would have known.'

'Yes, well, I do know, it's just that I didn't think it would ever really happen to me.'

'Are you cross with me?' Emily was looking for reassurance.

'How could I be cross,' Colin began to soften his tone. 'This is wonderful news.'

'Really? What about the extra mouth to feed?'

'My so-called friend, Ned, who's told you all about my bad attitudes, also told me, some time ago, that when my own child is born, I will be as moonstruck as he always is. I didn't believe him at the time, but I'm beginning to understand my friend better lately.'

'I'm so glad I married you,' Emily snuggled closer to her husband. 'I know you are going to make a wonderful father for our children.'

'And you're going to be a wonderful mother.' Colin responded to her caress, beginning to pull a pin from her hair.

'Should we go back to the mansion and tell your mother, and Aunt Vera?' Emily suddenly broke the mood.

'No!' Colin was not so easily distracted. 'We'll tell them tomorrow.'

'But don't you think . . . .'

Colin placed a restraining finger on her lips.

'You, my dear wife, could drive me half crazy if I let you.'

Emily brought her mind back to focus on the intensity of the moment, but for only a second, and then she broke into a smile. Tipping the end of his nose with her finger she spoke to him in a teasing voice. 'There's nothing I want more than a half-crazy husband,' she said.

THE MANSE

The first novel in

❧ The Heart Of Green Valley Series ❧

By Meredith Resce

John Laslett has just arrived in Green Valley as the
new parish minister, employed by the patron, Lady
Vera Wallace. At first it seems that the grand lady is
full of grace and her intention is to see to his every
need. However, there is something strange about the
housekeeper she has sent. Kate is efficient in every detail,
but John cannot seem to break through the cold exterior.
Something is wrong, he is sure, but he doesn't know
what . . .

Kate has a secret she doesn't want anyone to know,
especially the hateful new minister—the man who has
taken her father's place.

THROUGH THE
VALLEY OF SHADOWS

The third novel in

✤ The Heart Of Green Valley Series ✤

By Meredith Resce

When tragedy strikes, Christine Shore is certain that her life will never be the same again. Naturally, she considers shouldering the responsibility of caring for her orphaned niece and nephew—despite the family's assurance she is under no obligation to raise the children.

Jack Browning, the children's uncle on the other side, has nobly proposed to marry Christine for the sake of the children.

However, when presented with an opportunity to travel overseas, she chooses to let Jack care for his brother's family and find another woman to fulfill his hasty vow.

Unforseen circumstances lead Christine to question whether she has made the right decision, or whether she has let true love slip her by.